MW00812645

FLAMING
MODERATE

FLAMING
MODERATE

A RIVETING JOURNEY AND
QUEST TO SAVE DEMOCRACY

BO ROBERTS

Leigh Hendry, Editor

Headshot by Jerry Atnip

gatekeeper press™

Tampa, Florida

FLAMING MODERATE:
A RIVETING JOURNEY AND QUEST TO SAVE DEMOCRACY

Published by Gatekeeper Press
7853 Gunn Hwy, Suite 209
Tampa, FL 33626
www.GatekeeperPress.com

The editorial work for this book is entirely the product of the author. Gatekeeper Press did not participate in and is not responsible for any aspect of this element.

Library of Congress Control Number: 2023948832

ISBN (hardcover): 9781662943355
eISBN: 9781662943362

Table of Contents

Chapter I

WHY FLAMING?

It was 3 a.m. when the leaping flames from the burning cross in our front yard roused our household, along with that of our closest neighbors. The reprehensible members of the Ku Klux Klan were quiet like snakes as they came slinking across our grassy lawn to plant and ignite their instantly recognizable symbol of racism. As far as I was aware, this was the group's first official cross-burning in our small town of approximately 4,000 residents. Employing their standard weapon of intimidation, the KKK lit up our idyllic hamlet. The brightness of their fiery deed was a call to arms, bringing us flying out of our doors.

My close friend and neighbor, Sevierville stalwart and native son Johnny Waters had dialed the city's volunteer fire department before dashing outside. The firemen were there in no time, arriving in a somewhat stealthy manner without using the truck's wailing sirens (a detail that dawned on me later).

The burning wood was rapidly losing its power, the red-hot cinders fading as the firefighters (they were friends of ours and included several of Johnny's cousins) focused on extinguishing the cowardly work of the infamous Klan. This sign of the Klan's insidious presence, while essentially harmless, was somewhat unsettling. Until that very moment I hadn't bothered to take them seriously—despite the United Klans of America having established their Tennessee headquarters in Maryville, just 28 miles away. That was quite a miscalculation on my part, as this group's fire would become the first flame to singe my life.

The Klan emerged as a destructive element during the time that I was serving as the nation's youngest editor of a pair of weekly newspapers in Sevier County, Tennessee. Despite its location as the gateway to America's most visited national park, the Great Smoky Mountains National Park, Sevier County was still somewhat isolated, insulated and rural. However, the local government was in the throes of becoming more modern and professional in its approach to all aspects of its operations. At the time, its education system was also less than impressive.

As I was completing this book, I pondered whether to use the word "flaming" in the title. That consideration sparked a multitude of flame-related memories and reflections—both literal and figurative—that had affected and influenced my life. As a result, "flaming" made the cut.

My first significant, life-changing flame was the experience with the hate-spreading KKK. I chronicled the episode in detail in my first book, *Forever Young: The Youngest as a World's Fair President, Editor, Governor's Cabinet Leader & University Vice President.* Quick recap: It involved a continuing conflict of several weeks where the KKK attempted to incite support for violent action against the county's education leaders. They had made the monumental decision to integrate the schools. Naturally, I vigorously editorialized against the Klan's anti-integration nonsense. When the group held a rally on the courthouse lawn, I was the primary target of the Tennessee Grand Dragon's fanatical rant. Initially somewhat amused, I maintained my cool until he began assailing my journalism acumen. When he yelled that I "didn't know what was going on," I responded, shouting at the top of my lungs: "Do *you*?" That led to a stir that escalated toward borderline violence. At that point, my level-headed buddy, Johnny Waters, wisely suggested that we depart.

The Klan's intimidation tactics continued with threats and late-night phone calls to my home; an approach was usually quite effective for them. I continued to shrug it off though, as 'bullies being bullies' until their enthusiasm waned and they limped away in defeat. The Sevier County *News-Record* quickly published a statement authored by the Sevier County Ministerial Association, lambasting the KKK's actions while expressing full support for school integration.

A year later the flame burned again—figuratively speaking. After accepting a position in the communications field and relocating to Atlanta, I received a call from a *Life Magazine* reporter inviting me to lunch. He was working on a series about the Klan and wanted to discuss my recent interaction with them. When we met, I asked why he chose me? He showed me a copy of *The Fiery Cross,* the Klan's national publication. I was shocked to see a picture of myself on the front page. My photo was accompanied by a highly unflattering article identifying me as a "communist spy." We laughed, of course, and bonded as fellows-in-arms against the Klan.

My next "flaming incident" was three years later, but it also involved racial issues. I was in Washington, D.C., working in my role as Chief of Staff to Tennessee Governor Buford Ellington. Late in the evening on April 4, 1969, I received a message to call the Governor immediately. He broke the news about the assassination of civil rights leader Martin Luther King in Memphis. He explained that he was in the process of mobilizing the state's National Guard because he felt they would be needed to maintain order and quell potential violence.

With no flights departing D.C. at that hour, I booked the first available flight out the next morning. En route to the airport, I saw fires that had been set and people breaking into buildings. It was a city awakening to a tumultuous time; one that would mark a national eruption of unrest, strife and pain. With the plane gaining altitude, I looked down to see a landscape marked by flames and trails of smoke. It reminded me of the horror-filled images of World War II, and seemed inconceivable that this was occurring in our nation's capital.

I had a similar feeling when I reached the Governor's residence later that morning. The stately Georgian mansion had been transformed into a military command center with the Governor and his advisors in a position to direct a full-scale security operation. There were 4,000 Guardsmen on high alert. The state highway patrol and national guard leaders were monitoring the harrowing situation, relaying information to Governor Ellington. Though this wasn't my area of expertise, the Governor had asked me to stay on site with him. I observed these good, competent men (as it was 1968, there weren't many females in high-level government positions), fueled by adrenaline, performing admirably during an unprecedented moment in modern American history. As they were determining where to send which units, the National Guard's Adjutant General said: "I hope none of our boys get hurt." To which I quietly said: "I hope *no one* gets hurt." There was a momentary pause, and an uneasy silence. The collective head-nodding that followed seemed to infer agreement with my statement.

I'm not suggesting that my comment made a definitive impact, but, I do know that the Governor's all-encompassing response with the Guard on duty was receiving criticism in some quarters. Some felt that the Governor's response might be overreaching. However, today the record shows that there were no—as in zero—fatalities in the very state where King lost his life. Again, while not attempting to claim credit, I can say that I made an effort to douse a dangerous "flame" on an extraordinarily sad day.

The next major flame that would have an impact on my existence was a red-hot logo that would fire things up for the next 2800 days of my life. This flaming symbol would come to represent the most successful special category world's fair in U.S. history. I had the good fortune (on most days) to serve as president and CEO of the 1982 World's Fair in Knoxville, Tennessee, where the theme was "Energy Turns the World." The logo showcased the universe's primary source of energy: the sun at its hottest and most powerful.

It was a flame that deeply impacted my life for close to eight extremely intense years. During its 184 days, the Fair attracted some 11.4 million "energy" fanatics, making it the largest tourism event in the history of the southeastern United States...a record that still stands 40 years later. It was also an event that could not have happened without a cast of thousands. It took direct, sleeves-rolled-up, bipartisan action by scores of rare human beings, many of whom are noted in the penultimate column, "Celebrating Bipartisanship at its TN Best."

An abundance of details about the Fair and other stories are included in my aforementioned memoir, *Forever Young.*

These paragraphs are my take at sharing the actual, virtual and symbolic influences that factored into the use of the word "flaming." I realize that the word might mean something different to others than it does to me, and, if so, great. In particular, the word elicits emotions from friends in the gay community, as well as from their enemies. Their passionate desire to enjoy the same rights afforded to everyone else in a free society.

Interpret and define however and whatever flaming means to you. Influenced by every experience I've mentioned, it also means that no matter how frustrating situations may seem, or how hopeless efforts might appear, the flame has to be tended... if we want to keep it burning.

Chapter II

WHAT IS A MODERATE?

My definition of a moderate isn't simple, and I don't align it with a political party or ideology. If I had to pick one person whose life and career epitomizes the ideal moderate, I would undoubtedly choose the late, great United States Senator, Howard Henry Baker, Jr. of Huntsville, Tennessee.

Through my friendship with neighbor Johnny Waters, (yes, the same Johnny I mentioned earlier who shared the Klan experience), I met and enjoyed the privilege of becoming closely acquainted with Baker, the incomparable Scott County native.

Howard and Johnny, law school classmates at the University of Tennessee, were both deeply interested in politics. Not long after receiving his J.D., Johnny returned to his hometown of Sevierville, hung out his shingle, and began practicing law. He also dove headfirst into the proverbial political pond by launching a Republican primary challenge against an entrenched incumbent. The invincible Rep. Carroll Reece, who had already served 13 terms, was running again for Tennessee's 1st Congressional District House seat in 1958. Young Johnny, who campaigned voraciously, received scads of media attention by incorporating a live elephant into his appearances. The pachyderm, which was there to reinforce Johnny's bona fides as an intrepid Republican, seemed to thoroughly enjoy the process too. And, while Johnny made many new acquaintances, it was not nearly enough to unseat the indomitable Reece.

Baker's life in the political arena was somewhat assured by virtue of his birth. His father, Howard Baker, Sr. served seven terms as the congressman representing Tennessee's 2nd Congressional District (from 1951 until 1964 when he died in office). He was succeeded by his wife, Irene, who was appointed to serve the remainder of her husband's term. Knoxville Mayor John Duncan, Sr. was elected to the seat and took office in 1965. Meanwhile, Howard, Jr. ran for the U.S. Senate in 1964 and lost to Democrat Horace Bass, before taking another shot at it in 1966 when he emerged victorious defeating the Democratic nominee, incumbent Governor Frank Clement. Baker's campaign manager during both races? His friend, classmate, and fellow U.S. Navy veteran, John B. Waters, Jr.

In January 1967, Baker was sworn in as Tennessee's junior senator, the same month I was sworn in as a cabinet member and Chief of Staff to re-elected Governor Buford Ellington (his first term as governor was 1959-1963; governors could not succeed themselves in Tennessee at that time).

I was often in our nation's capital on state business where I would occasionally meet with Senator Baker. We both understood that we were always available—just a phone call away—to discuss any issue or deal with any mutual problem or opportunity regarding the state.

I relate all of this not to infer that I was important, but to note how fortunate I was to know, and frequently observe, the finest public servant in Tennessee's modern era. That we were members of different political parties didn't matter; not because we were friends, but because that was Senator Baker's modus operandi. He was receptive to anyone who wanted to improve either the state or the nation.

It was such a pleasure to watch Baker be celebrated by his colleagues when they elected him to lead their party, first as Minority Leader (1980-1981) and then as Majority Leader (1981-1985) of the Senate.

While it's practically impossible to summarize a legend's career, I can cite two examples that impart the flavor of this man. The first is a small, Tennessee, regionally related matter that occurred in 1969. The young senator was a part of an energized, excited Republican party working to form a new government following Richard Nixon's election to the presidency. The Republicans eagerly anticipated a return to the White House after eight arduous (to the GOP, at least) years. Baker invited me to join him for breakfast in the Senate dining room, and after a few pleasantries over our first cup of coffee, he asked my opinion regarding the Nixon administration nominating Johnny Waters as Federal Co-chairman of the Appalachian Regional Commission (ARC). The ARC was a federal endeavor created by President John F. Kennedy to bring additional money and incentives to the 13 states with counties in the Appalachian mountain region, an area that had historically been economically depressed. The commission was administered by the 13 governors (or their designee, which, in Tennessee's case, was me) and a presidentially appointed Co-chairman. Funds were distributed on a project-by-project basis to supplement ongoing federal-state programs.

Ironically (and I was never sure if Senator Baker knew this or not), I learned about the program while at UT, when a Sevier County delegation hired me as a part-time consultant to raise money for a new library. Sevier County's library at the time consisted of a half-of-a-floor on the second story of Sevierville's Masonic Temple. While there had never been a private fundraising effort that raised more than $5,000, I convinced Waters to lead a volunteer non-profit Foundation to raise $60,000 in matching funds. We raised more than $100,000 when we found that the ARC program would supplement the public investment with an additional $30,000. That bonanza allowed us to construct the library and to purchase enough books to be recognized as one of the best small libraries in the state.

Needless to say, I was delighted by Senator Baker's query. Not surprisingly, Johnny accepted the job at which he performed admirably. He had a bi-partisan, down-home, common sense way of doing business. We had such a blast that the rest of the states, and his staff grew weary of hearing the Sevier County Library story. But, it was the perfect illustration of what the ARC program could accomplish. We never took advantage of our positions, but we garnered every single dollar possible for Tennessee's Appalachian region, which included almost 70 per cent of the state.

The second example involved an issue that affected the entire country as well as the world.

In the summer of 1973, Senator Baker was appointed as the top minority member of a special Senate committee named to investigate the charges against the Nixon administration, dubbed the "Watergate Affair." As the committee's vice chairman, Baker was expected to be the administration's defender, and the person who would demonstrate that the allegations were little more than a Democrat-led conspiracy.

As the hearings progressed and troubling information began to emerge, Senator Baker, a civil but skillful inquisitor, posed a question that would ultimately define his career as it reverberated around the world: "What did the president know and when did he know it?" He would later describe Watergate as "the greatest disillusionment" of his career.

Following three distinguished terms, Senator Baker chose to retire from the Senate in 1985. He was later drafted back into service by President Ronald Reagan, who implored him to return to Washington as his Chief of Staff. When the Iran-Contra affair engulfed the Reagan White House, the President realized that it was going to take an extremely seasoned diplomat to rescue his sinking ship. Senator Baker was the answer to his prayers. In answering President Reagan's call, Baker shelved re-entry at his law firm, Baker Worthington, along with his consideration about launching another presidential bid.

Three years after he had restored respectability to the Reagan White House, President George W. Bush asked for Baker's assistance, and appointed him as Ambassador to Japan in 2001, a position he held until 2005.

Baker's law practice, founded by his grandfather in Huntsville in 1888, later merged with iconic Memphis legal giant, Donelson & Adams. Baker Donelson is today one of the largest law firms in Tennessee with offices in 22 cities throughout the Southeast.

These brief paragraphs, which barely brush the brilliance of the Senator, don't begin to document his singular contributions to the U.S. and the world. His most famous admonition was this: "Listen to the other side, because, occasionally, they may be right!"

He was widely known as "The Great Conciliator" for his numerous bi-partisan achievements. That label was referenced in 2014 when then-Senate Majority Leader Mitch McConnell of Kentucky announced Baker's passing to senate members. In his remarks, McConnell described Baker as "one of the senate's most towering figures," and said: "He will be remembered with fondness by members of both political parties."

The ideals that Baker brought to American life have had a fresh opportunity to blossom again in recent years through the Howard H. Baker, Jr. Center for Public Policy, now elevated to the Baker School of Public Policy and Public Affairs at UT-Knoxville. An institution dedicated to the Senator's principles of knowledge and accomplishments through civil discourse, the Baker School provides an outstanding example of American political civility. Mining personal political dirt against an opponent as one's most formidable weapon in a campaign was not an acceptable approach in Baker's book. His actions were positively refreshing then, and certainly would be seen as such now. It's rewarding to see this effort, under the able guidance of Dr. Marianne Wanamaker, to educate new leaders who, regardless of party affiliation, are committed to dignified interactions and the old-fashioned political practice of simply reaching across the aisle to solve problems. The Center launched a terrific podcast in 2022 featuring two distinguished Tennessee leaders, both of whom are cited many times in several columns included here. Former Governor Phil Bredesen, a Democrat, co-hosts the podcast with former Republican Governor Bill Haslam in a forum appropriately entitled, "You Might Be Right." It's not coincidental that both were successful, non-partisan mayors of Nashville and Knoxville, respectively, before each served eight years as particularly effective governors. I would proudly label both as "moderates." Their podcast continues to enjoy a robust following.

Others making noble efforts to keep the "flames" of hope alive include Gray Sasser, the son of Jim Sasser, another moderate Tennessean who served three senate terms. Gray is the Executive Director of the Vanderbilt Project on Unity & American Democracy, working with an impressive team of researchers, faculty members and political leaders at Vanderbilt University to reframe public discourse. Also, David Plazas, the Nashville *Tennessean* and Gannett's Tennessee editorial director, adds to the effort with his ongoing campaign as a voracious defender of civility as an essential element in politics.

Have I answered the question, *What is a Moderate?* Maybe not. But, by relating some traits of my hero, I feel that I have outlined the actions of a person worthy of emulation.

* * *

In my lifetime, our state has been blessed with a line of formidable leaders who have shepherded Tennessee to national and international prominence. Though none ever claimed to be perfect, and certainly none were, their traits of reasoned leadership cast a radiant light.

On my party's side, we had Senators Albert Gore, Sr. and Junior, Jim Sasser, and Governors Frank Clement, Buford Ellington, Ned McWherter, and Phil Bredesen. On the Republican side, we saw Senators Howard Baker, Fred Thompson, Bill Frist, Lamar Alexander, and Bob Corker, along with Governors Winfield Dunn, Lamar Alexander, Don Sundquist, and Bill Haslam, all of whom were fine examples of results-oriented, accomplished, and, dare I say, moderate officeholders. They were architects of a strong state, built on a bedrock of sound fiscal management.

There were a plethora of other people involved in pushing the Volunteer State toward solid achievements and progressive policies, as well. Those I have had the pleasure of knowing, who also made outstanding contributions in their own spheres, would include the acclaimed state Comptroller Bill Snodgrass, Finance and Administration commissioner, deputy governor, state treasurer and U.S. Senator Harlan Mathews, Speakers Jimmy Naifeh, John Wilder, Beth Harwell, and Ron Ramsey; and not to mention as a significant link from Baker to Dunn, Alexander and Sundquist, the Memphis attorney, state official and namesake to Baker's law firm, Lewis R. Donelson, III.

Because of personal exposure and relationships, I would also note the considerable contributions of Congressman John Duncan and his family, former Minority Leader and Deputy Governor Jim Henry in East Tennessee, and my buddy, Congressman Steve Cohen from Memphis. I think most readers would agree that the hazard of making lists such as these is cliff-leaning. I've possibly tilted over that cliff, but I can say with conviction that all of the people mentioned here are beyond deserving. It is well-documented that many had tremendous impact nationally and internationally.

I confess that I have not included any current officeholders because, frankly, the jury is still out, still sequestered. Many appear so driven by partisan ideology—- rather than ideas and ideals—-that they have inspired me to share my thoughts in these pages.

What and maybe, *who is a moderate*, is in the eye of the reader and the beholder. I hope you'll join me on this journey, consider these decades of ideas, and, if you don't concur with my conclusions, please know that I know "you may be right."

ON THE CAMPAIGN TRAIL

Young upstart Johnny Waters uses symbolic GOP

elephants for his lively, but unsuccessful campaign against Tennessee

1st Congressional Congressman Carroll Reece.

(Photo from Waters Family Archives, 1958)

ABOARD AIR FORCE ONE

Longtime top Baker aide Tom Griscom, left, listens to President
Ronald Reagan, along with White House Chief of Staff Howard Baker
and Deputy Chief of Staff Ken Duberstein, far right.

(Photo courtesy of Tom Griscom)

SWEARING IN–U.S.

Supreme Court Justice Potter Stewart swears in Johnny Waters to his

ARC office with Waters' wife Patsy holding the Bible.

Witnesses are Senator Jennings Randolph, Congressman

Jimmy Quillen and Senator Baker.

(Photo courtesy of Cyndy Waters)

SENATE HEARINGS

Johnny Waters, center, at his U.S. Senate Hearing concerning
his presidential appointment as Federal Co-Chairman of the
Appalachian Regional Commission, flanked by Congressman Jimmy
Quillen, left, and his senate sponsor, Senator Howard Baker.
(Photo provided by Cyndy Waters)

FRIENDS IN HAPPY TIMES

Senator Baker was the link for friends to gather during
the swearing-in ceremony of new Appalachian Regional
Commission Federal Co-Chairman Johnny Waters from Tennessee.
From left to right, Senator Jennings Randolph from West Virginia,
Waters, Baker, and U.S. Supreme Court Justice Potter Stewart.
Democrat Randolph's state was the only one of the 13 member states
that was 100% within the ARC borders. Not surprisingly, the senators
were close personal friends as well as colleagues.
(Photo courtesy of Cyndy Waters)

CONGRESSIONAL CELEBRATION

Powerful gathering to celebrate the swearing-in of Johnny Waters
as Appalachian Regional Commission Federal Co-Chairman.
Shown, left to right: 2nd District Congressman John Duncan of Knoxville
(1965-1988), 1st District Congressman Jimmy Quillen of Johnson City, TN
(1963-1997), and Waters, Sevierville, TN with Senator Howard Baker,
Huntsville, TN (1967-1985) and Waters' father, John B.Waters, Sr.
(Photo provided by Cyndy Waters)

SENATOR BAKER AND THE MEDIA

In an undated photo, the media surrounds the Senate Majority Leader
at one of the many "crisis of the day" sessions.
*(Photo courtesy of the Baker School at the University
of Tennessee-Knoxville)*

HISTORIC MODERATE PODCAST

Former Democratic Governor Phil Bredesen and former Republican
Governor Bill Haslam host a regular podcast, produced by the Baker
School of Public Policy and Public Affairs at the University
of Tennessee-Knoxville. In a salute to the school's namesake,
the podcast is appropriately named, "You May be Right."
(Photo courtesy of Baker School at UT-Knoxville)

Chapter III

WHO AM I?

When sharing this book's working title, *Flaming Moderate,* with friends, many first had a look of surprise, then a smile...then a slight, knowing nod of appreciation. It was the best way I knew to state a quixotic desire to *return, recreate, recycle, hope for, demand, and expect....* a nation to avoid extremism. We can hold differing viewpoints and still accomplish something.

As a Democrat, I crave the days when good candidates from both parties fought like hell to win an election. Then win or lose, they would work for what was best for *our families, our city, our state, our nation, and our world.* Is that too much to ask today? My answer to that is a strong "no." It's essential to keep passion and energy alive in the search for fearless candidates. We need those unafraid of alienating extremists. Let's move 'em to the middle....let's accept moderation, but not mediocrity. It's possible to encourage greatness by casting wide nets of consensus in the search for real results.

This book is my attempt to share thoughts and opinions, developed over a lifetime, and expressed primarily through op-ed columns published during the past 20 years. The issues were sometimes national, sometimes statewide, sometimes local. In almost every instance, I was searching for solutions. My preference has long been to comment on problems *only* when I could offer a solution, no matter how far-fetched it seemed.

So, Who Am I?

Well, I'm not gay.

I'm not black.

I'm not Jewish.

I'm not Hispanic, Asian, or Middle Eastern.

I'm not a member of any organized religion.

I'm neither liberal nor conservative.

So, who am I?

Just an older white guy, who tries to appreciate, or at the very least respect, all of the things noted above that I am not. I feel fortunate to have friends, who are gay, black, Latino, Jewish, and other persuasions or circumstances. I admire and value my friends, not because they fall under any of the labels above, but because they're my friends, who happen to be who they are.

Like them, I'm far from perfect. I learned early in life that the person who believes they're the smartest person in the room often proves how dumb they are.

I try to remember that the more I learn, the more I have to learn...no one can ever know it all.

I do love life, so I want to stay active and engaged while exploring ways to improve *life, standing, understanding, decision-making, tolerance, politics, and respect.*

That's why I'm a moderate. I'm not in the middle to be average, but to conquer differences together, by taking the best ideas and use them to improve *all of the above.*

I say *flaming* because it expresses my passion to continue trying, no matter how frustrating the divisions, the intolerance, the bigotry, or the height and number of hurdles.

The late, renowned North Carolina State basketball coach Jim Valvano implored, as he was succumbing to cancer at the age of 47, that we continue to battle his formidable disease after he was gone: "Don't give up, don't ever give up."

This book is my effort to communicate a similar premise. Most of these columns concern politics and the challenges of government and issues at the local, state, national, and even, international levels.

I hope you'll enjoy this journey. And, regardless of either your ideology or your party affiliation, please consider participating in the ongoing quest for flaming moderation.

Chapter IV

PRELUDE

Kudos to songwriters for crafting a melodic framework for us that enriches our lives. With just a few words and notes, their work helps us start and end our days with turns of a phrase that stick in our minds, whether we want them to or not.

Two songs that I kept hearing as I wrote this book were:

"Clowns to the left of me, jokers to the right.... here I am stuck in the middle with you." Stealers Wheel recorded the song in 1972. Gerry Rafferty and Joe Egan penned the lyrics, which were actually intended as a parody of Bob Dylan's style and as a dismissive tale about a music industry party. The record sold millions in England, then the U.S. and in Canada. If I could change the words a bit, the overall theme of my book would be:

Clowns to the left of me, jokers to the right
Here we are, stuck in the middle with us

I first wrote a column deriding partisan extremism in 2013. I referred to that song and melody then, and it continues to come back to me every time I think about how we can infuse American politics with moderation.

To some, moderate may sound neutral, pointless, or even mediocre. But, when properly applied, it is anything but those adjectives. That brings me to the first half of the title here, *Flaming*. The reason behind both brings Aretha Franklin to mind. Can't you hear her wailing the word?

"RESPECT........R...E...S...P.E.C.T"

That hit, written by Otis Redding and released in 1967, epitomizes the word classic not to mention that it deftly alludes to women's issues. My paraphrasing would be:

RESPECT.......... Equals .R...E...S...U.L.T.S

To me, the lack of results in America is what keeps me pushing, helping and driving our need to focus on one goal: RESULTS.

If a group or an individual is spending energy and time trying to prove how liberal or conservative they are, if they're more concerned with bona fides than benefits, then there will be no *RESULTS.*

Some think we need to form a new, third party where moderates can convene to right our national ship and restore democracy. I wholeheartedly disagree. It would require too much time and energy to deal with the logistics and the minutiae. Each party should deal with its shortcomings while thinking broadly enough to incorporate positions that will lead to *RESULTS*.

Recent developments by the Trump wing of the Republican Party have widened the right to include a dangerous group of hoodlums advocating violence and the threat of violence. That element of the party is not interested in right or left. They have infused fear as an element of control. That fear is now physical, in addition to being psychological. Their extremism has infected our political system, and makes coming together to resolve problems and meet opportunities vastly more difficult than ever before.

Things were tough enough prior to this mob mentality being energized to legitimize one person. Again, I use the phrase "flaming" because no matter how hopeless the cause seems, we must do what we can, when we can. We must marshall every resource to reach a common goal: **R.E.S.U.L.T.S.**

I have had the privilege of knowing a few songwriters in my life, two of whom I met after moving back to Nashville years ago. Both are members of the Songwriters Hall of Fame, a nod to their unbridled creativity which has brought such immeasurable enjoyment to millions around the world.

One, Tony Arata, was the subject in a column not included in this book. Tony introduced me to the "real" Music City by inviting me to Songwriters' Nights, primarily at Douglas Corner.

While an editor of a magazine our company published, Tony practiced his songwriting craft during his time off. He had an early hit that is a celebrated classic today: "The Dance," recorded by Garth Brooks in 1989.

An illustration of the extreme impact that a song can have was clearly demonstrated in a *Sports Illustrated* feature story. It centered on the widows of two baseball players who perished during spring training in a 1993 boating accident in Florida. Prominently highlighted in the story was the fact that one of the wives dealt with her overwhelming sorrow by playing, "The Dance" on repeat. The *SI* writer prominently highlighted several stanzas of Tony's song. When I took the magazine to Tony, he was not aware of it. Imagine how many others in the world are comforted or inspired every day by the words of a songwriter?

The other Hall-of-Fame songwriter, Tim Nichols, is one of the most modest guys I've ever met. He deflects every conversation back to the inquirer when the topic of music arises. Among the memorable songs Tim has written is "Live Like You are Dying" (co-written with Craig Wiseman), a monster hit for Tim McGraw that was named *Billboard's* #1 country song in 2004. I've heard multiple stories about how that song reminded listeners to cherish their time on earth and put a priority on spending time with others.

As you journey through this aggregation of legends and tales of yore, you might occasionally find yourself humming:

CLOWNS TO THE LEFT OF ME, JOKERS TO THE RIGHT
HERE WE ARE, STUCK IN THE MIDDLE WITH US
 and
RESPECT..........
R...E...S...U.L.T.S.

Chapter V

SETTING THE POLITICAL STAGE

INCONGRUENT THRILL OF VICTORY

NOVEMBER 4, 2002

I leaned over the railing of the indoor balcony at Nashville's downtown Hilton Hotel, taking a moment away from the raucous party occurring with a small cadre of friends and colleagues.

I was reflecting on the exceptional moment we had just experienced, which was the result of the indefatigable drive of a bespectacled, often brash, but super sharp Jewish guy from Memphis. Looking at the lobby five stories below, I saw hundreds of ecstatic Democrats. They had gathered there to share in the fruits of a consequential victory achieved by a once-divorced, Harvard-educated New Yorker, whose wife had the temerity not to change her maiden when they married. The 59-year-old businessman had just been elected governor of Tennessee.

I shook my head thinking about the confluence of these two campaigns by two people who would have significant impact on Tennessee's history. They had each established lasting legacies, though neither of them would have passed the traditional checklist of norms for Volunteer State candidates.

In the campaign suite, Shelby County State Senator Steve Cohen was as relieved as he was delighted. His 20-year crusade advocating for a lottery benefiting education had just culminated in a citizens' vote to amend the state's constitution. The campaign received 895,532 "yes" votes in a runaway, 15-point, constitutional-changing victory. I had helped Steve a bit during the lottery drive, and joined him in celebrating with some close friends, among them the uber-talented, unbelievably loyal, research-machine that is Marilyn Dillihay. She would move to Washington to work with Steve when he was elected to represent Tennessee's 9th Congressional District in 2007.

The 2002 celebration of Nashville Mayor Phil Bredesen's victory was jubilant, noisy and wildly joyful. He received 837,284 votes in a tight, three-point win over GOP nominee, Congressman Van Hilleary. We were particularly elated for Bredesen's political strategist, guru Dave Cooley, as he had experienced the thrill of three victories and the agony of three defeats with the brilliant Bredesen. Following an extremely successful business career, Bredesen wanted to share his vision and leadership with the people of Nashville and Tennessee. Cooley, as one of my savviest fellow Roane Countians, went on to serve as Deputy to the Governor, before returning to the private sector following his boss's commanding re-election victory in 2006.

Over the years, I have been a part of, or witnessed, countless political victories and losses. I have immense esteem for those who have placed themselves in a public position to be scrutinized, criticized, and denounced, or less often praised, by becoming a candidate for any office. Occasionally a friend, or a friend of a friend, might ask me to meet with them as they mull a run for office. My first question is always: "Are you prepared to lose?" Their reaction is universally the same. They would look at me incredulously, as if to say: Why would you ask me such a negative question?

My response is without fail: "Because I have been in too many rooms with crying spouses, upset children, grieving parents, and furious close friends who were mourning the loss of an election where so much time, energy and faith was invested." Politics is, in the end, very personal. There are winners but also losers, and that possibility should be considered before a decision to run is ever made.

It. Is. Very. Personal.

That's why I have such deep admiration for those willing to stand where lightning is sure to strike.

The best personal advice I ever received was early in my career as Governor Buford Ellington's Chief of Staff. Toward the end of the term, those who had gained even a sliver of recognition were speculating that they might run for governor. I was somewhat flattered when a few folks hinted that I should consider the possibility myself. I received a call from the famously charismatic John Jay Hooker, Jr., whom we had vigorously opposed in the first campaign I worked on—the fiercely fought Democratic primary race of 1966. We had gotten to know one another and had actually become friends over the course of four years. John Jay said: "Bo, I hear you are thinking about running for governor?" I replied: "Highly unlikely."

Hooker added: "Well, let me give you one piece of friendly advice: Can you afford to lose?" It took me less than 10 seconds to consider my answer, as the idea of being unemployed with a young family, a mortgage, and no secret trust fund at hand, to reply with a laugh: "You just hit the nail on the head, John Jay! Thank you!"

That's why I respect those who commit to being a candidate.

That conversation was one that floated across my brain at 9 p.m. on that November election night in 2002. During my moments of solitude on that balcony, I was close to elation at the thought of the unlikely possibility of savoring two victories simultaneously. It was the first time I could remember that happening, and would probably be the last.

(Since changing the constitution to permit the lottery, Congressman Cohen can bask in the glow of his two-decade drive to enrich Tennessee education. More than two million students have received scholarships since the lottery was established.

Following his election as governor, Phil Bredesen's future accomplishments in that role could only be described as phenomenal. One was working hand-in-glove with the former Chattanooga mayor and later Republican U.S. Senator Bob Corker to convince Volkswagen USA to locate a plant in the Senator's hometown. More than 5,000 Tennesseans are now employed there.

Bredesen's re-election was a remarkable stamp of approval as he triumphed in every county in the state, all 95 of them.

That 2006 election was the last time a Democrat was elected to a statewide office in Tennessee.)

THE CRUSHING AGONY OF DEFEAT

NOVEMBER 7, 2000

The faces of my best friend and three of his colleagues were etched with pure anguish as they came trudging into our home for an "after party" on that dismal night 23 years ago.

Emmett Edwards, my brother-in-arms, and UT football seat mate, his buddies and myself had departed the "watch party" for the 2000 presidential election earlier that evening. The outcome looked like it was going to be an unmitigated disaster. Vice President Al Gore's entourage had been headed toward downtown Nashville prepared to deliver a concession speech. But, just as quickly, they halted, perplexed by what they were hearing. Word was rapidly spreading that the results were inconclusive. That indecision would initiate weeks of legal maneuvering based on the counting of votes in Florida, a process that could be known as the "Battle of the Hanging Chads."

That night, those who worked in Nashville's national headquarters, experienced a flash of renewed hope that Gore might still prevail.

But Edwards and his group were devastated because they were part of the staff of the Tennessee Election Headquarters.

The reality was this:

Had Al Gore won his home state, he would have been the president-elect of the United States.

The indecision down in Florida would have been inconsequential if a majority of the voters in Gore's home state had turned out for their "favorite son." I told Emmett and his friends that they didn't lose the election, and Gore didn't lose Tennessee because of the campaign's effort in the Volunteer State. Gore had actually lost the state during the past several years when he and his staff had neglected to "dance with the one who brung you."

First, let me offer some perspective: The Clinton-Gore ticket won Tennessee in 1992 with 933,521 votes, and while that was less than 50%, it was still enough to beat incumbent President George H.W. Bush (42%) and Independent candidate Ross Perot (10%). In 1996, the 909,146 votes cast for the Clinton-Gore ticket amounted to 47%, still enough to carry the state over Senator Bob Dole and Ross Perot, 5% this time when he ran as the Reform Party candidate.

In 2000, GOP nominee George W. Bush received 1,061,949 votes to VP Gore's 981,720 (47%). There was no strong Independent candidate that year. So, despite the vice president getting the most votes that a Gore ticket had ever received, he still lost by 80,000 votes.

I'll offer two rather insignificant examples of why Gore might not have fared well in his home state.

The Tennessee State Museum was preparing to host a major art exhibition involving a valuable collection to be shipped from

France. Anticipating complications with shipping and customs clearance, the museum called a friend on the Vice President's staff. The reply they received was, in essence: Sorry, but we can't be seen providing "special treatment" to Tennessee. There was nothing inappropriate about the request, nor would it have helped reduce expenses; the ask was simply to alleviate a bureaucratic blockage. They moved on to GOP Senator Lamar Alexander's office where they quickly received the necessary assistance.

* * *

The other example involved former Tennessee Governor Ned McWherter, a figure beloved by Democrats and many Republicans, as well. Someone in the national campaign office had requested special assistance from McWherter, so he graciously traveled to Nashville to meet the officials in the national office. After a considerable amount of time waiting for the meeting, he finally departed, stopping by the Tennessee campaign office to say hello to some friends before heading back home to Dresden. (When I heard this story, it reminded me of the time that Vice President Gore reportedly asked Governor McWherter why he always stayed at the White House with President Clinton when he traveled to Washington instead of at the Vice President's residence? The Governor said: "Well, Al, you never asked me.")

I'm certainly not saying that Al Gore is not a good man. I'm simply pointing out that an accumulation of impressions of indifference stacked up in his home state, one after the other over an eight-year period. These served to dilute a lot of passion. Tennessee voters should have been "all in" for their native son to become the fourth American president from the Volunteer State, but when the votes were tallied, they told a different story.

My words of solace to the dedicated Gore guys nursing their wounds in our living room that evening might have assuaged some of their pain, while the excellence of the red wine offered as an effective pain killer. Regardless, the disappointment of that heartbreaking defeat would never be completely erased.

CELEBRATING THE CALL OF VICTORY

Having just received word that the Tennessee Lottery
vote was declared a landslide win by the Associated Press,
State Senator Steve Cohen, the lottery's steadfast shepherd for
20 years, enjoys a jubilant moment with, left to right, Gloria Houghland,
the author, and super staffer Marilyn Dillihay
in the Downtown Nashville Hilton Hotel.

COMMITTEE DUTIES

Congressman Cohen makes a point during one

of the many House of Representatives' committee meetings.

(Photo courtesy of Congressman Cohen's office)

PRESENTING A PRESIDENT

Congressman Steve Cohen introduces former

President Bill Clinton at a 2016 campaign stop in Memphis.

(Photo courtesy of Congressman Cohen's office)

POLITICAL PARTNERS

Governor Phil Bredesen and political sage Dave Cooley
together in a recent photo. Cooley, who orchestrated Bredesen's
two successful gubernatorial and Nashville mayor's races,
also served as Deputy Governor.

(Photo courtesy of Dave Cooley)

FRIENDS FOREVER

Emmett Edwards and the author meeting at Morton's,
The Steak House. Edwards, a top executive in the Tennessee Gore
for President campaign, also held top positions
in the administration of Governor Ned McWherter,
the 1982 World's Fair and the administrations of former
Nashville mayors Bill Purcell and Karl Dean.
He lost his battle with cancer in 2012 when he was 59.
(Photo courtesy of Cory Mason, then GM at Morton's)

48

Chapter VI

THE AUGHTS
COLUMNS 2005-2009

This journey begins with the thoughts introduced in the Prelude: The imperative need for leaders to work together for the greater good. With each column reflecting my reaction to the events occurring at the time of their writing, I believe that one will easily see a consistent call for cooperation not confrontation. I wish I could say that the net effect changed either our state's or the nation's political direction, but I can only state that they undergird my strong desire that hope will always prevail. Some of those who seek the same outcome have suggested creating a new party. But, I see that as an energy-sapping effort that would induce minimal movement of the "political needle."

*Let's start the journey and replenish the energy by revisiting the columns. All but one of these was published in the Nashville **Tennessean** and often in other publications, as well. Written over the period of three decades, I chose those that dealt directly with* *political issues. I also selected those which addressed the number one government responsibility: Education. I included columns concerning huge investments of public funds, along with issues that would become political. I believe that these cumulatively demonstrate the benefit of "flaming moderation."*

MAYBE WE NEED ANOTHER HELICOPTER RIDE

AUGUST 1, 2005

(At a time when Tennessee governor Phil Bredesen was dealing with some critical issues at the state level, I felt that it was important to pause, take a break and reflect upon the considerable contributions that made him so successful as mayor, and illustrated why he was elected and would make a formidable governor.)

MAYBE WE NEED ANOTHER HELICOPTER RIDE
By Bo Roberts

There was no strain as the helicopter carrying 1200 Nashvillians took off and flew us into the future.

Most of us were mesmerized as the then-mayor, Phil Bredesen, piloted the virtual helicopter six years into the future. We looked out in amazement to see a new Nashville arena, and, wait, across the street a new downtown hotel…and, wait, can you believe it, a sparkling new Country Music Hall of Fame. And, this was truly hard to imagine, people walking and spending money on Broadway all the way down to Second Avenue. And, and…wow, what a ride.

It was April 4, 1994 and my partner had dragged me to yet another State of Metro address hosted by the Greater Nashville Chamber of Commerce. It was always a fun event when

51

one saw a lot of friends, but also predictable and a bit boring. Not on this day, though. This day we saw a vision of a mayor, who would never be pigeonholed as a huge sports fan, seeing the new sports and entertainment facility as the key to a major overhaul of Nashville's physical downtown and our community's lifestyle.

I kept thinking of this ride a few days ago when reading and hearing all the carping and whining about spending money on the Nashville arena and on the coliseum that houses the Titans. We've already forgotten what a catalyst those facilities were for cleaning up "Lower Broad" and the industrial slum across the river from downtown. Note that the coliseum wasn't part of the Mayor's helicopter ride that day, because the Oilers/Titans move to Nashville wasn't yet on anyone's radar screen.

Luckily, when the opportunity came, Mayor Bredesen was ready to act. There were some bumps in the road, but in the end, nearly 60% of Metro voters said "Yes" to the NFL.

I'm not saying there's anything wrong with raising questions about the maintenance costs of these facilities, but for God's sake, folks, let's not lose perspective about what they have done for this city. In hindsight, maybe the operating contracts could have been a little tighter. But isn't it amazing how hindsight always rears its head after the opportunities are taken?

Maybe it would have been good for Nashvillians to have taken a virtual helicopter ride when the NCAA brought March

Madness to Nashville this year. Thousands of people from throughout the country spent millions of dollars and had a great time (even better if their team won) in the arena, the restaurants, the hotels, visiting the Country Music Hall of Fame and on and on. Or when more than 60,000 celebrated New Year's Eve in Nashville while they attended the Music City Bowl and spent millions of dollars to fill hotel rooms that are normally empty during that time of the year. These are just two events in the past few months.

So, it takes some money to maintain and operate these entertainment jewels, but even with a hockey lock-out last season, these facilities are probably the most important thing to happen to Nashville in the last two decades. They not only brought pleasure, but have generated millions of dollars and thousands of jobs.

Maybe, just for perspective, we should take just a cursory look at some other recent capital expenditures or authorizations:

$9.7 million for "moving, setting up, operating and leasing of relocation space for courthouse offices." Had to have it, but that's a lot for temporary space.

$25 million for an underground parking garage on the new courthouse site; great because I look forward to the new park adjacent to the courthouse;

$14.9 in deferred maintenance for schools, obviously needed.

$10 million a year for sidewalks; I enjoy the ones near me, but they don't necessarily create revenue.

$19.4 million for "fleet purchases" (that's cars and trucks); obviously we have to replace old fire and police vehicles and other necessary equipment.

And on and on. I'm not saying any of these expenditures are not needed, but, again, let's keep our perspective. The total authorized capital budget for 2004 was $242.3 million. I'm sure every dollar was necessary, but I would almost bet that virtually all of that money together won't generate the dollars and jobs like the arena and the coliseum.

Even if you don't care for sports or concerts or ice shows or Mayor's Night Out with school children, I hope you would agree that Nashville is a more vibrant place now than it was before we had these catalysts for change.

Thanks, Phil Bredesen, for taking us on that helicopter ride, but even more for having the vision to see what could happen and the fortitude to make it happen. Maybe the whiners should take a helicopter ride. If they're not up for that, maybe they should consider taking a hike instead.

THE FACES OF ENERGY BEHIND THE MUSIC CITY CENTER

JUNE 1, 2006

(At the time, a consideration of a new convention center in Nashville would, at $600 million, make it the largest public project in Tennessee history.)

THE FACES OF ENERGY BEHIND THE MUSIC CITY CENTER
By Bo Roberts

Like me, I'm sure that you have often heard the ubiquitous phrase: "They said." Quite often the person citing "they" is hard pressed to name the actual source that said something, anything or, even nothing.

As the effort to educate Middle Tennesseans about the benefits of the proposed Music City Center moves forward, we might lapse into the

"they said" trap without actually knowing the "them." Fortunately for us, "they" are real folks, volunteers who are giving hundreds of hours to shape the future of Nashville. And I mean giving literally, because they are getting paid zero, zip, nada for their efforts. Why? Well, we'll get to that in a moment.

"They" started by serving on the Music City Center Committee, selected by Mayor Bill Purcell to study and recommend whether Nashville needs more convention center space and after a 15-month effort, recommended a new 1.1 million square foot convention center with a price tag of $455 million.

But, again, who are "they" and why did "they" give their time to this study and the resulting coalition to implement the center? Let's take a look at the three main leaders:

Marty Dickens—Came to Nashville in 1999 as head of BellSouth Tennessee; born in North Carolina, degrees from East Carolina and Georgia State universities. Community/civic involvement includes: past chair of the Nashville Area Chamber of Commerce as well as the Nashville Convention and Visitors Bureau, board of directors of the YMCA, the Boy Scouts and Belmont University.

Randy Rayburn—Came to Nashville in 1975; owns Sunset Grill, Midtown Café and Cabana's restaurants; Milan, TN native, University of Tennessee graduate. Community/civic involvement includes: Taste of Nations, Nashville's Table, boards of Nashville Symphony, the Belcourt Theatre and the Nashville Convention Center.

Ralph Shultz—Came to Nashville in 1996; president and CEO of Adventure Science Center; Louisville, KY born, Chattanooga raised, University of Tennessee graduate. Community/civic involvement:

Leadership Nashville, Leadership Music, the Domestic Violence Intervention Center and Nashville Youth Leadership.

Now that you have more concrete information about the "they," let's go back to why. With more than full-time responsibilities and presently involved in an indefatigable number of other community projects, why, indeed, did these people add to their already full plates?

"First, we couldn't turn down Mayor Purcell when he asked us," Dickens said.

"Then, the more we got into it, we quickly realized that this was a crucial decision in Middle Tennessee's future." While they were all quick to note pertinent facts and figures, Rayburn summed it up in terms most important to taxpayers: "The best thing is that folks outside of Nashville will pay the tab."

Their passion for their subject shows through, even as they deflect credit to the dozens, and now hundreds, of other volunteers who have given, literally, as many hours as they have. That would be a lot, because between the three of them, one can easily tabulate 1,500 hours of free consulting labor on behalf of our city...and, the meter is still running.

But so far, these three convention-center musketeers have taken the lead and the majority of the heat in the court of public opinion. Folks, you may be for the Music City Center or you may have changes that you think should be made or you may be against it completely, but please appreciate the time and effort that your neighbors have freely given.

As they have said in many different ways, they love this city. So, while no good deed may go unpunished, in this case, at least when you hear someone say "they said"...well, you'll know who they're talking about.

LIGHTNING NEVER STRUCK

JULY 1, 2006

LIGHTNING NEVER STRUCK

By Bo Roberts

I left the early-voting location with trepidation. Surprisingly, lightning didn't strike.

I thought immediately of my deceased mother, hopeful that she wasn't watching from above. My just-completed, totally un- precedented action would really disturb her: I had just voted in a Republican primary!

As a life-long Democrat, I confess to voting on rare occa- sions for a Republican candidate in a General Election, but to cross over and vote in the Republican primary? No way. At least until now.

The rationale that brought me to this monumental (and I suspect one-time), uncharacteristic behavior was thinking about Tennessee's tradition of electing senators of whom we could be proud. Whether a Democrat or Republican, I think most would agree that our U.S. senators over the past few decades have been smart, decent men who served with dignity while never embarrassing us and, for the most part, they took rea- sonable positions rather than being bound by totally partisan ideologies.

Certainly we could have disagreed with some of their votes and positions, but when surveying the complete body of work of Howard

Baker, Al Gore, Jim Sasser, Fred Thompson, Lamar Alexander and Bill

Frist, we can say that their leadership and national stature served Tennessee well.

It was that political history that precipitated my bold step this election year. Going against the political option of voting for the easiest candidate to beat in November, I voted for the man I thought would make us proud if elected. That man was Bob Corker.

I have had the privilege of knowing Bob Corker for the past 20 years. He is a decent, bright, no nonsense guy who has a track record of serious accomplishment. If elected, I believe he will be a forceful, yet reasoning leader.

Having no heated rivalries in this year's Democratic primary gave me a certain level of comfort in crossing political boundaries. To assuage my guilt and as an act of forgiveness, I did write in the names of Phil Bredesen for Governor and Douglas Henry for State Senator, two men I greatly admire. My late Mom, once voted the Yellowest of Yellow Dog Democrats in all of the Volunteer State, would probably be okay with this. With the brilliant and charismatic Harold Ford, Jr. in the race as the assured Democratic nominee, and, if successful next week, Bob Corker as the

Republican nominee, I'm looking forward to a robust campaign with two outstanding candidates, who are also good men. To my Democratic friends, I can safely say that if one is inclined to cross over, it wasn't fatal this time, but I don't want to make a habit of it.

Regardless of my vote and regardless of the outcome in November, Tennessee will be well represented in the U.S. Senate once again.

C'MON TEACHERS, GET REAL

OCTOBER 1, 2006

C'MON TEACHERS, GET REAL
By Bo Roberts

It's easy to get "furiouser and furiouser" watching educated people kicking, not just looking, a gift horse in the mouth.

I don't know who volunteered to anonymously donate $400,000 for incentives to help in producing better results in some of Metro's most troubled schools, I know that they must be a generous and dedicated citizen. However the "who" is not the central issue here—what matters even more is that a majority of Metro's teachers who participated in a recent Metro Nashville Education Association vote on accepting the gift, ultimately decided not to accept the contribution without bothering to offer a simple thank-you in the end.

And, please don't get the impression that I am anti-union. In fact, I am anything but, My father was a decades-long union member, and I have seen the good that has resulted from union advocacy over the years; yet, there have been abuses during the unions' storied history; and I would undoubtedly place this action squarely in that category.

Because I have a background in fundraising with public institutions, I am also aware that not all donors give with pure motives and that not all gifts can be accepted, particularly if the terms are odious. But, from what I understand after briefly studying this issue, the offer to the teachers was driven by a desire for results. C'mon teachers, show us where there are true devils in these details. You may quibble about small points, but what you have really done is throw the 'philanthropic baby' out with the incentive-laden bathwater.

Maybe entertainer Dolly Parton got it right when she pledged to aid students in Sevier County, where she grew up; offering $1,500 to every two-person team in the eighth grade that completed high school. Dolly's current, and most recognized program, is to provide books every month to children from birth until they reach first grade. Every county in the

Volunteer State is now participating. Clearly, no one asked the Metro Teachers' Union to vote on that issue, thank goodness. Since the benefits of Dolly's program accrues directly to the kids, I am going to take a wild guess and say that if parents had to vote on it, the support would have been overwhelming—-even if some found minor details with which to quibble.

When I heard the MNEA vice president say to Metro School Board Chair Marsha Warden's query that she should "consider the extent to which your questions interfere with MNEA's representational rights," before he closed with: "The ice is thin," I sensed I was seeing the root of the problem. I believe the ice may be thinnest of all for his position. It's far better to do what is best for the kids than it is to stand on procedural stuff squabbling over a power issue.

My hope is the generous donor doesn't do what most would under these circumstances and tell the school system to "forget it." I also hope that the more enlightened educators will muster some leadership and renounce the rejection of a well-intentioned attempt to address some of Metro's public school problems.

And, unfortunately, maybe this unfathomable action opens our eyes to why some of those problems exist.

THE GOLD RULES, VOTERS PAY

FEBRUARY 1, 2007

THE GOLD RULES, VOTERS PAY
By Bo Roberts

It's not exactly true that "every Tom, Dick and Harry" is running for president, but it seems like it. There are, so far, at least two Toms, two Johns, a Sam, a Joe and a Mike. They are joined by Dennis, Duncan,

Barack, Rudy, Mitt and Hillary. Who knows who else might surface (a Newt? an Al?).

Now if you, an op-ed reader of the *Tennessean,* have trouble immediately thinking of all the last names, think about the poor folks who don't have the time or inclination to do so. It will take a lot for these candidates to become known. In fact, most experts say that it will take between $50 million to $100 million to be truly viable in a national primary. Then these candidates will have to run as a presidential nominee. Most knowledgeable observers predict that each nominee will spend $500 million on the general election.

There's something wrong when it takes more to run a presidential campaign than it would to buy the Tennessee Titans, the Dallas Cowboys, and the New York Yankees. Actually, the $2-$3 billion dollars which will be spent between now and November of 2008 could buy a lot of things, but, unfortunately it won't necessarily buy America an educated electorate.

We all share in the blame for this situation. As we demand 10-second sound bites, 30-second commercials and one-liners that define our candidates we are selling ourselves short. Eventually we may dig into the candidates' platforms to ferret out more substance, but how many of us will take the time to do so? Not many, I think.

Is there a better way? I would hope so. However, it seems that every time we take the appropriate steps to put limits on the spenders and the spending (e.g. Feingold-McCain Election Reform Act), campaign experts quickly devise ways to skirt the restrictions while escalating the dollars. We see a pattern of over exposure and under communication. Maybe one place to start would be with the media, who can pledge to devote more time and space to discuss, in a civilized manner, actual issues. I think we have all reached our threshold of entertainment with the spin-meisters who shout over one another. Some responsible media already offer us some sane options, but, sadly, few watch and read.

To effect real change, it's going to have to come from us, the voters.

Someday we will get fed up and say: enough already! Let's put limits on time and money; let's hear and see what the candidates actually have to say and find out who they are and what they believe. A pipe dream?

Well, not if every Tom, Dick and Harry......

SHANI'S SONG

APRIL 1, 2007

(The tragic mass shooting at Virginia Tech University caused an uproar nationally and dominated press coverage for at least two weeks. Little did we know that such events would become weekly, almost daily events over the next 16 years, and seeking solutions needed and still needs bi-partisan action.)

SHANI'S SONG

By Bo Roberts

Think of all the songs and melodies that have echoed in your mind and wouldn't go away. It's a common experience.

The one that stuck in my head over the past few days didn't even have a melody; it didn't even have words, just a title: Shani's Song.

Those words have been reverberating in my thoughts recently because a former colleague, named Shani, was my personal, most direct link to the tragedy at Virginia Tech. Shani was a Hokie through and through.

Shani McNamara came to work for our company straight out of Virginia Tech. Bright, attractive, eager to make her first job a successful experience, she was an energetic and quietly confident young woman. From 1992 to 1994, our public relations clients adored her, both as a professional and as a person.

I, along with all her colleagues, loved her too. She left us to marry fellow-Hokie, Patrick Bowers.

Now the mother of two Hokies-to-be, Shani and her family live in Midlothian, VA. We communicate via email, and it was her email asking for prayers for the "Hokie Nation," that evolved into "Shani's Song," and she doesn't even know it.

I also had a few sports-related encounters with the Hokie Nation. The first was during the miserably cold and rainy, in-augural Music City Bowl at Vanderbilt Stadium, when VTU walloped Alabama. Then in 2003, a couple of buddies and I traveled to the beautiful Virginia Tech campus in Blacksburg to see a Thursday night football game against Texas A&M.

We sat with 85,000 Hokie fans in a driving rainstorm gen-erated by Hurricane Isabel, and watched the Hokies romp once again. In 2004, in a specially arranged season-opening college game at FedEx Field (home of the Washington Redskins), the Hokie Nation made up at least 90 per cent of the more than 90,000 (dry) fans. But for a disputed offensive pass interfer-ence call, the Hokies would have ruined the season for eventual national champion Southern Cal. All of "us Hokies" were upset; Shani and I shared the disappointment via email.

These and other Hokie memories came flooding back when I first heard about the unbelievable carnage in Blacksburg. After reading Shani's email, I couldn't get the thought out of mind that my life and the lives of dozens of other Nashvillians would have been much less enriched had we not known and experienced the bubbly, positive energy that she brought with her to Nashville.

Who knows how many lives won't be touched, how many friendships won't be formed, how many positive contributions won't be made because of this tragedy? Any murder is a reprehensible crime, but when the victims are primarily young people it seems even more so. I know there are many in Nashville who grieve every day from the loss of a loved one to murder. Like the Hokies who won't be with us, we all miss out on what might have been.

I wish I could write the song or the melody, but maybe Shani's Song is not just about tragedy; maybe it is a song telling us all to treasure our friends, our loved ones and to fully appreciate life's experiences. Thanks Shani, for being my friend and for providing your song of appreciation. I don't know if the Hokie Nation is better for it, but I know I am.

(Shani Bohlin now lives in Steamboat Springs, Colorado. She added a nursing degree when she was 32, and during the pandemic earned her MBA and is an entrepreneur, starting a prosperous regional concierge nursing practice called Blue Skies Nursing.)

NASHVILLE SHOULD BOLDLY LEAD THE WAY IN SCHOOL DIRECTOR SEARCH

MARCH 1, 2008

NASHVILLE SHOULD BOLDLY LEAD THE WAY IN SCHOOL DIRECTOR SEARCH

By Bo Roberts

A couple of years ago, Rip Van Winkle awakened after 100 years of sleep to see what the world had become.

As he rubbed his eyes, so the story goes, Van Winkle was amazed by the wondrous changes that had occurred during his century of somnolence. Automobiles, airplanes, spaceships, telephones, radio, television and the internet left him gasping with excitement.

Then he visited a 21st century classroom, where, at last, he found a rectangular room, with a teacher and blackboard up front and students seated at desks. Finally, he thought, something that hadn't changed!

I came across this illustration last year while doing some research on education for Nashville's mayoral campaign. While looking at multitudinous studies, this image kept floating back into my consciousness. Now, as we watch Metro Nashville wrestle with a selection of a new director to lead our public schools, the Van Winkle image has emerged again.

Metro Nashville has a tremendous opportunity to offer innovative educational leadership while making a selection that could change the course of education for, perhaps, the next half-century. But, we can't be bound by the traditions of conventional educational thinking. We cannot continue to do the same thing over and over hoping for different results.

If ever there were a time for "thinking outside the box;" it is now.

Don't be beholden to a process which limits selection to those who apply. There may be some outstanding candidates, but why should we look only at a set of people (applicants) who want to move up the ladder or have "qualified" by doing the same thing over and over again, either here or elsewhere?

Don't be constrained by the traditional "qualifications" of educational administration. The search committee should consider establishing some criteria that that might include success in a field other than education. Who would a Warren Buffet, Bill Gates or Martha Ingram look for to address this challenge?

Finally, our director should have both passion as well as compassion. The ideal candidate should be passionate about: results, children, teachers, parents and should possess the sensitivity to discern the challenges faced by each of those constituencies.

Most importantly, the finest candidate may not even know they are a candidate; they may have to be sought out and convinced that Nashville is a place ready to embrace innovative ideas as well as fresh directions. Let's go recruiting, here at home and on a national level. We are in search of a leader who will inspire all interest groups to join together in finding a better way.

Maybe, just maybe, if ole Rip revisited Nashville after a second nap of 10 years, he might be astounded at what has changed in education here.

This is Nashville's moment; hopefully, it will not be our final opportunity to boldly lead the way.

BEWARE OF WHAT YOU ASK FOR; TWEAK DON'T REVISE TRANSFER OF GOVERNMENT POWERS

JUNE 1, 2008

BEWARE OF WHAT YOU ASK FOR; TWEAK DON'T REVISE TRANSFER OF GOVERNMENT POWERS
By Bo Roberts

"In its wisdom, the General Assembly".....is a sentiment that could be an oxymoron to some. However, over the long haul it usually applies.

The discussions of changing Tennessee's constitution to address the transfer of powers should a governor become unable to perform his/her duties has led, in my mind, to a "rush to elect" a lieutenant governor.

Let's slow down, think this through and examine the alternatives.

While thinking about the General Assembly and its wisdom, I thought back to December of 1972. A Republican (Winfield Dunn) was governor and some Democrats wanted a more politically active Comptroller of the Treasury. When the House and Senate Democratic Caucus met to nominate (and essentially elect) the state's constitutional officers, a campaign was swiftly implemented to nominate Floyd Kephart, a bright, young political activist, for the position of Comptroller. Such action would have booted Bill Snodgrass from office; a man who was widely recognized as one of the top fiscal government officials in the nation. Prior to the legislative convention, five Democrat senators joined members of the Republican party to support

Snodgrass. When the votes were counted in January, 1973, a majority of the General Assembly "in its wisdom" had made Tennessee history and returned Snodgrass to office.

State government's tallest building in Nashville is now named the William R. Snodgrass Tower for a reason....Bill's career of nearly five decades was a testament to what good and effective public service is all about.

His work continues in the man he mentored, John Morgan. In fact, with one brief exception in the 1980s, Tennessee has been blessed with enlightened, stable leadership in all of its constitutional officers. There hasn't been a scintilla of impropriety, let alone scandal.

My point is this: the system is working. Though there may be an occasional bump in the road, we have all benefited from a well-run state government that manages to squeeze the most out of each precious tax dollar.

Part of the reason for that is the strong fiscal policies of the constitutional officers, and the fact that Tennessee is a "strong-governor state." One reason the office of governor is so important is that it is the only statewide-elected office.

The "tick bite furor" which led us to address this question had, until last year, never come up. What to do about the transfer of a governor's power if the chief executive becomes temporarily incapacitated?

Governor Phil Bredesen (who was away from the office but never out of control due to illness) appointed a prestigious Advisory Committee to review the question. Headed by able Attorney General Bob Cooper (the state's AG selection, by the way, is unique in the nation as this position is selected by the Tennessee Supreme Court), the group, which included the speakers of both houses of the General Assembly, former Supreme Court Justice A. A. Birch and former governor Ned McWherter, went to work.

Their final report presented an orderly and simple way to address the issue, which could be requested by the governor or initiated by the attorney general and taken to the State Supreme Court to rule.

A problem then arose: If the Lt. Governor takes over for even a short time, he/she must relinquish the post of Speaker and Senator, allowing someone else to be elected....a major price to pay for what could be a part-time job.

That's when the talk about an "elected" Lt. Governor initially began, opening an unfortunate Pandora's box of misguided reasoning in the clamor for other elected officials (attorney general, secretary of state among others). The state should proceed cautiously down that very dangerous road.

Because one of the strengths of a well-managed state government is continuity, an interruption in a governor's plan and direction with the inclusion of another elected official is not a wise choice. That official (Lt. Governor now, or elected) may be well-meaning, but it could still be an interruption.

Some say, let the Lt. Governor be selected by the governor and they then run as a ticket, similar to the Federal model of a vice president. Might work, but would be a major change and fraught with getting the best person politically on the ticket, not necessarily the best person to carry out, as yet unspecified, duties.

I suggest we consider formalizing the office of Deputy Governor, which is an unofficial, yet very symbolic name first given to Harlan Mathews by former Gov. McWherter and continued by every governor since. It would probably take a tweak in the constitution (instead of a major shift) and allow the business of government to continue relatively seamlessly for a period of time (probably set a limit, after which a vacancy could be declared and the normal succession of a vacant office could take place).

There may be other and better ways to address this situation (which hasn't happened yet, but could). Mainly, I implore our esteemed General Assembly to dig deep for "your wisdom." We truly need it now.

HIGHER ED FEELS HIT

NOVEMBER 1, 2008

HIGHER ED FEELS HIT

By Bo Roberts

When does enough finally become too much?

Tennessee may be reaching that point in one significantly critical area as the state budget belt tightens in response to an economic downturn.

That area: Higher education.

As one who has been privileged to work in higher education (University of Tennessee) and to consult with the nation's sixth largest system of higher education (Tennessee Board of Regents), I have some knowledge of the many dedicated, hard-working, penny-pinching leaders we have in this state. They have taken their lumps in the budget cuts as have other areas of state government. But, unlike other state agencies, they have a resource for offsetting some of the pain: student tuition.

But, when do we reach the point of diminishing returns? We are getting perilously close.

A bit of a reality-based, historical check here: When first elected, Gov. Phil Bredesen had to address a disastrous budget situation, which he handled with aplomb. He dealt with the hemorrhaging TennCare system, wrestled the budget demons into balance, and, when the economy was better, he introduced

76

progressive programs for moving Tennessee ahead with education at the forefront.

I believe, and a recent statewide poll indicates I am not alone, that Gov. Bredesen has acquitted himself quite well.... during the good times, and particularly during the recent tough times. Who better to steer us through this economic morass?

His priorities prevailed during the budget reductions, with only K-12 surviving actual cutbacks. That's as it should be. However, I think another priority should be considered if the bleak economic forecasts continue, and that is public higher education.

How much more should students and their families pay? Again, as one who has followed the ups and downs of public higher education for decades, the rule of thumb was two dollars of state appropriation to each dollar of student tuition and fees. That rule began eroding in the 90's, and reached the "tipping" point in fiscal 2003-04 when, for the first time, students were paying more than the state appropriated.

During the past 10 years, tuition and fees increased more than 150 per cent, while state appropriations increased less than 40 per cent.

Unfortunately that gap continues to widen.

What does all this mean? To me, public higher education in Tennessee is in danger of losing ground....territory that will be more and more difficult to recover. Despite such mitigating factors as the lottery-funded scholarships, assistance to non-qualifying students is declining.

We can speculate and theorize all we want, but my reality check as a first-generation, GI-bill-supported graduate of a public institution who has benefited a lifetime from that opportunity. I don't want others to miss out on a similar chance because they can't afford it or because programs have been drastically reduced.

I only ask that as future budget adjustments are made, that the state's leaders carefully consider the long-term ramifications that additional cuts will have on this vitally important part of Tennessee's potential and its future.

MAYBE A TENNESSEE COLOR PURPLE COALITION?

JANUARY 9, 2009

MAYBE A TENNESSEE COLOR PURPLE COALITION?
By Bo Roberts

When almost 30 Nashvillians gathered at our house last month, we had at least three things in common:

- We were all supporters of President-elect Barack Obama,
- Not one of us was a Davidson County native,
- We each hoped for an inclusive administration seeking bi-partisan solutions to the monumental challenges now facing America.

As one of the more than 4,500 "Obama House Parties" held throughout the nation during the second weekend in December, our group was

impressively diverse: multi-racial, multi-party and multi-generational, from teachers to investment bankers to the recently unemployed. Our "charge" was to gather input for the Obama transition team.

It was an enlightening, inspirational two hours on a cold, gray Saturday afternoon.

We themed the event "A Blue County in a Red State," since Davidson was just one of four Tennessee counties that gave

Obama a majority. Reflecting later, I thought about the group's common desire for bi-partisan solutions, and realized that the Volunteer State had much to offer the president-elect and his team. Listening closely and broadly would be their first task.

Consider creating a "Color Purple" coalition and include the congressmen from two of the "bluest" counties, the brilliant Jim Cooper from Nashville and the enigmatic, energetic Steve Cohen from Memphis. I could see them teaming with two "red" representatives with extensive and successful stints in local and state government in Tennessee: Senators Lamar Alexander (former two-term governor) and Bob Corker (former Chatta-nooga mayor and former state finance commissioner).

The blue mix from the U.S. House of Representatives would acknowledge the early campaign loyalty of Cooper and Cohen, who represent Tennessee's largest metropolitan areas, and are fully aware of the recession-laden suffering of an urban area.

The "red" mix from the U.S. Senate, offers two men who sur-mounted challenges as chief executive officers of their state and city, respectively. Both senators concluded their terms with a long list of accomplishments, high approval ratings and track records of reaching "across the aisle" to solve problems and meet challenges. Their voices are those who understand the complex realities of what works best at those governmental levels. Their hands-on experiences could prove invaluable in crafting a bi-partisan stimulus plan.

The current issues which our country is facing are neither red nor blue; they are, however, dauntingly color-blind. Like the other Middle Tennesseans gathered in our living room, I am inspired by President

Obama's transformational message of hope, his reservoir of intelligence, and his calm, yet firm sense of courage. He has clearly pointed out that he can't do it alone; he wants and needs our helping hands.

Part of our collective suggestion is that he consider the highly-qualified, down-home input that a purple-colored coalition would provide. God bless you for hearing our voices, Mr. President, Please keep listening.

BRILLIANCE+WISDOM+TRUST= HEALTH CARE SOLUTIONS

JUNE 1, 2009

BRILLIANCE+WISDOM+TRUST=HEALTH CARE SOLUTIONS
By Bo Roberts

As an astutely brilliant former Speaker of the Tennessee House of Representatives once told me: "Neither party has a monopoly on ignorance;" his statement framed one of my earliest, most significant political lessons.

The current furor over the nation's health care reform is an excellent demonstration of that Speaker's insightful adage. The idiocy of the right, railing about death panels and abortions, is equal to that of the left when it claims that the U.S. government alone can supply the panacea to this massive problem. The left's rejection of rational compromises, which its members characterized as off "center," can only be termed childishly immature.

Hopefully, national health care reform will stem runaway costs while assisting the almost-40 million uninsured citizens. Most Americans probably agree that adjusting our healthcare system is far overdue.

For those who concur, it doesn't take long to realize that there are no simple, effortless answers. Imagine this: the U.S. House's 1,100-page draft bill currently being circulated has a five-page Table of Contents. Five pages! Even if one is moderately intelligent, where would they find the time to become fully conversant on this highly complicated issue?

Well, folks, an approach I've adopted in the past and, I believe will work again is to listen to one of the brightest and most capable individuals I've ever known. That person? Tennessee Rep. Jim Cooper, a man who possesses the wisdom and humility to apply the necessary and correct solution.

I have long-marveled at Cooper's ability to speak knowledgeably, and with unmatched depth and perception, about virtually any subject. A self-professed "nerd," he is graced with self-deprecating humor, along with that rare ability to take matters, but not himself, seriously.

I don't always agree with every position he takes, so don't automatically dismiss this as a puff piece. For example, I disagree with, yet totally respect, his recent decision to reject "government pork" for Davidson County. For Cooper, that particular call was a matter of principal and fiscal discipline.

The left's unwarranted attacks on the Congressman and other "Blue Dog" Democrats are as infuriating as they are unjust. After all, this is the same man who developed a health care reform plan in the early '90s that was much more prudent than the one advocated by Hillary Clinton. Had Cooper been appropriately heard then and had we all listened more attentively, we might have averted this crisis today.

As we absorbed the President's presentation on health care, I reflected upon what Cooper told me before Obama's speech: "It's time for some adult supervision."

Well said. We elected an extraordinarily intelligent president; now, I am hopeful that Mr. Obama is savvy enough to recognize that judgment is acquired both in small doses, as well as in gigantic servings.

So let's put some actual adults in charge, set ignorance aside and let wisdom reign. And, when the crucial vote comes, I feel comfortable with Jim Cooper holding my proxy.

CORRECT CHOICE, RIGHT TIME

SEPTEMBER 1, 2009

CORRECT CHOICE, RIGHT TIME

By Bo Roberts

The proverbial statement from the Book of Ecclesiastes," To everything there is a season," always circles back to remind us of its wisdom.

Such is the case with the recent action taken by the Tennessee Board of Regents (TBR). Last month, the TBR tapped John Morgan, the state's current deputy governor, as chancellor of the nation's sixth largest system of higher education.

Both the time and the person were right.

Public higher education in Tennessee is facing a future fraught with serious issues. The greatest challenge lately has been in attempting to balance the public's unquenchable desire for better education with the available, but dwindling financial resources. Those demands have been assuaged primarily through increases in student tuition fees.

Those who have either worked or been involved in the state's public higher education first felt the tremors of trouble nearly a decade ago when income from tuition fees exceeded the Tennessee General Assembly's allocated appropriation. The gap has continued to widen since that time.

Earlier this year, Governor Phil Bredesen and the General Assembly convened a special legislative session aimed specifically at addressing the issues facing education in the Volunteer State. A significant change was made in public higher education when the group collectively determined that emphasis should shift from funding based on enrollment to funding based on results (graduation success).

What better time for the TBR to make strategic changes than right now?

In selecting a chancellor with a profoundly different background, the Board has chosen a person of integrity and wisdom with outstanding leadership skills. John Morgan "grew up" in state government, under the tutelage of one of Tennessee's most respected and talented public servants, the late State Comptroller Bill Snodgrass, whose name now adorns state government's tallest office building.

Morgan, who succeeded the esteemed Snodgrass as state comptroller, has provided wise and sound counsel to the state and the state legislature in a reserved, thoughtful, bi-partisan manner for many years. As deputy governor, Morgan was the chief architect of the education plan adopted during the special session. Not surprisingly, that plan has led to a $500 million federal grant, setting Tennessee apart as a newly minted, national-leader in innovation.

Many readers will recall the appointment of former State Senator Tommy Garland, a republican from Greeneville, as TBR chancellor in 1985. The selection of that adept and admired legislator was also viewed, at the time, as a "non-traditional" choice. Yet, Garland acquitted himself with aplomb during the five years in which he held the post.

Yes, always "..... there is a season..." And, in my view and in the opinion of many others throughout the state, *this* is the season which called for the correct man at the right time. John Morgan is an inspired, enlightened choice to lead six universities, 13 community colleges and 26 technology centers into the tumultuous decade which awaits. If we're smart, we'll allow him to begin the job without further distraction.

VII. THE TERRIBLE TWEENS AND TEENS
COLUMNS 2010-2019

POSSIBLE WAY TO STOP THE ENGLISH ONLY MADNESS
APRIL 1, 2010

POSSIBLE WAY TO STOP THE ENGLISH ONLY MADNESS
By Bo Roberts

During the current session of the state legislature, I have found it embarrassing to watch the asinine attempts of a dozen lawmakers as they have worked, once more, to sully the reputation of the Volunteer State.

I am referring to the proposed driver's license tests in English-only legislation (SB0063/HB0262). This bill is not only insulting, but is a slap in the face to those (including our governor, business leaders and, apparently, every one of the gubernatorial candidates) who have toiled diligently to bring new jobs to Tennessee through their outstanding industrial recruiting.

The idiocy is exacerbated by the Arlington, Va.-based Pro-English advocacy group, which is known for its racist viewpoints, and is the primary funding force behind this latest effort (they tried, well-funded but failed in Nashville).

I was even more upset when these out-of-state instigators attacked a friend of mine, who also happens to be one of the nation's top corporate leaders. That leader is Chris Karbowiak, who was recently named Chief Administrative Officer for Bridgestone Americas, one of our country's leading corporations which happens to be headquartered in

Nashville...as in Tennessee. Chris is not only one of the top executives in the country, she is actively involved in Middle Tennessee's non-profit community, currently serving as Chairman of the Board of the Music City Bowl and on the board of the Tennessee State Museum Foundation, among many others.

Karbowiak was verbally assaulted, primarily by rabble-rousers from outside our borders, because she had the audacity (ne courage) to speak out against this small-minded legislation...a bill which, if passed, would clearly send the wrong message to all of the 740 foreign-owned companies in our state that provide more than 100,000 jobs, including our newest neighbor Volkswagen, and companies who are considering bringing much-needed jobs to Tennessee. She's tough enough not to let these anonymity-clad barbs disturb her. But, as her friend, it does distress me as well as others.

What to do? I believe there may be an alternative which could prove quite effective in curbing just this type of legislation. My suggestion is to have an enlightened legislator (and there are many) introduce a resolution that all written and oral communication circulated by members of the general assembly must be in CORRECT ENGLISH ONLY. I'll bet every teacher in the state would support this effort. But, the main benefit of such a resolution is that it might potentially shorten the length of the legislative sessions by more than 50 per cent!

All state citizens would benefit; even those vocabulary-challenged members who might actually have to take the time to learn something new. Whether it's this idea or not, let's divert support from the actions of our learning-impaired and election year-pandering legislators who are tarnishing the great state of Tennessee.

CLOWNS AND JOKERS SQUEEZING THE MIDDLE GROUND

FEBRUARY 1, 2011

CLOWNS AND JOKERS SQUEEZING THE MIDDLE GROUND
By Bo Roberts

Clowns to the left of me, jokers to the right
Here I am, stuck in the middle with you

The chorus from the 1972 Stealers Wheel hit, co-written by Joe Egan and the late Gerry Rafferty, keeps echoing in my head as I've observed the frightening, politically divisive landscape which has erupted in Washington and Nashville, eroding the long-established tradition of fairly civilized discourse.

Not only are reasonable people having difficulty reaching appropriate and rational decisions, they are now being attacked for even conversing with those on the other side of the political aisle.

Two specific examples from 2010:

Clowns to the left of me

*When Rep. Jim Cooper voted against an early version of the Health

Reform Act he was immediately maligned by those on the left for (in their view) having abandoned basic Democratic

92

principles and for not supporting President Obama. Threats were made and the search began to find someone to oppose him in his next primary race. As one of the first public officials in Tennessee to support Barack Obama, the presidential candidate, and, as an acknowledged expert on health care reform, the vilification of Cooper was woefully undeserved.

Jokers to the right

*Sen. Bob Corker, after considerable research not to mention documented expertise, offered to work with the majority party to determine the best approach for determining and crafting much-needed financial reform legislation. He was immediately denounced by his colleagues on the right for having the audacity to act as consort with the enemy. An email disseminated by the U.S. Chamber of Commerce at the time urged recipients to contact Senator Corker and let him know that he should oppose any proposals made by the opposition party. Though unsure how my name got on the organization's email list, after forwarding a copy to the senator, I added them to my blocked sender's list, relegating their future communications to the spam file.

Just as the wisdom of good folks is not licensed exclusively to any single party, the first dictum of politics says: Neither party has a monopoly on ignorance. Perhaps we could all glean more wisdom from the seemingly banal lyrics of popular music:

Trying to make some sense of it all
But I can see it makes no sense at all

Through the years, Tennessee has been blessed with its fair share of measured and sensible legislators, office holders who were willing to put what was best for the state above what was most advantageous for them or their party. Hopefully, when the contentious, alienating, mean-spirited posturing wears thin, we will still have enough remaining level-headed lawmakers "stuck in the middle" to deal intelligently and equitably with the issues which truly matter to this state and to the nation. If they will step up, we can proudly repeat the refrain:

Here I am, stuck in the middle with you.

WHO LEADS WHO

Congressman Jim Cooper of Tennessee's 5th
Congressional District said his teamwork with Chief of Staff Lisa
Quigley was successful because he did "whatever she said."
The former congressman ably represented the 5th District from
2003-2023, after representing the 4th District from 1983-1995.
Following the state's redistricting of the 5th, Cooper did not run
for reelection in 2022. Nashville/Davidson County is now represented
by congressmen from the 5th, 6th and 7th districts,
none of whom reside in Nashville.

WORLD LEADER

Bob Corker made quite an impact in his two terms (2007-2019)
as a Republican U.S. Senator from Tennessee, including serving as
Chairman of the influential Foreign Relations Committee.
A successful businessman, Corker was also a notably productive
mayor of his hometown of Chattanooga (2001-2005).
He was well-known as a fiercely independent, plain-spoken leader,
who was not shy about describing the antics of the Oval Office
inhabitants as comparable to those that might
be found in an "adult daycare center."

STATE NEEDS NEW EMPHASIS ON HIGHER EDUCATION

MARCH 29, 2012

STATE NEEDS NEW EMPHASIS ON HIGHER EDUCATION
By Bo Roberts

Where does public higher education stand in the pecking order of priorities in the Volunteer State?

Not very high, I'm afraid.

In the past decade we have seen major shifts, some good and some bad, in efforts to provide a quality post-secondary education for Tennessee's students.

I had the privilege of being involved in one of the good things in higher education 10 years ago when I assisted then-state Sen. (now U.S. Rep.) Steve Cohen in the lottery campaign following Cohen's 20-year push to bring it to a vote. My reasons for involvement were many, but the primary one was to see that our state enjoyed the same type of opportunities that Georgia had derived from its HOPE scholarship program.

Those benefits included keeping more of the best and brightest students within our borders and providing opportunities to many who otherwise could not afford college. When first rolled out, the lottery HOPE scholarships here provided an average of 60 percent of the cost of public higher education.

While the amount has increased, alas, it now covers only about 40 percent of those costs. Why? That's another side of the story.

Fiscal year 2004-05 was figuratively a red-letter day in our history, when for the first time ever, state support of our colleges and universities was less than the tuition costs to Tennessee families to send a student to college. As illustrated so clearly by the graphic accompanying education reporter Julie Hubbard's recent story in The Tennessean, tuition went up as state appropriations went down.

The stark figures are: In the past 10 years, appropriations to our colleges and universities went down $231 million (a 33 percent decrease) while tuition increased $436 million (a whopping 76 percent increase).

As a part of the 2010 special session on education reform, one of the items included was a little-noticed paradigm shift in the way public dollars are allocated to our colleges and universities: The priority was changed from the number enrolled to production (read degrees). Other things were included, but what is now called "outcome-based" was central to the appropriations formula. This major change, to me, was one of the good things that has happened in the past 10 years.

The new challenge is to show our colleges and universities (and our students and parents) that higher education is important in this state.

To the credit of the last several governors and general assemblies, no matter what the economic challenges were, they kept K-12 funding at or above its base. That's a good thing, and should not change. We saw encouraging signs of support for higher education in Gov. Bill Haslam's budget message.

What's next? If we are going to achieve the level of success and greatness I think this state is capable of, we must move support of public higher education up the ladder and draw a line in the sand: Higher education is important, and we will now make our priorities K-16. It's high time.

METRO "SUGAR" MAKES THE TAX MEDICINE GO DOWN EASIER

JUNE 1, 2012

METRO "SUGAR" MAKES THE TAX MEDICINE GO DOWN EASIER

By Bo Roberts

Most of us are familiar with the lyrics from the famed '60s Disney musical film, Mary Poppins: "Just a spoonful of sugar helps the medicine go down, the medicine go down..."

The "medicine" I'm referring to is the current proposed property tax increase in our fair city while "the sugar" is something I have enjoyed ever since moving to Nashville more than two decades ago. That brand of "sugar" is specifically called "Metropolitan Government." As we celebrate 50 years of the wise decision made to merge our city and county governments, we should be aware of how beneficial that change was to our collective pocketbooks.

When I moved here from Knoxville, the value of the home I purchased was higher, but the taxes were less than I had been paying (when combining the Knoxville city and Knox County rates of more than 20 years ago). If one had moved here at that same time from either

Memphis or Chattanooga, they would have had a similar experience.

100

These relative cost savings have occurred during the course of Nashville's five-decade governmental metropolitan endeavor.

Based on the Tennessee Comptroller of the Treasury's latest report and updating it to 2011, here is what the figures show:

- Chattanooga/Hamilton County 24% higher
- Knoxville/Knox County 20% higher
- Memphis/Shelby County 78% higher (gulp)

These compelling numbers reflect an efficient, effective form of government, as well as the bold leadership skills of most of the city's mayors along with their prudence as good managers plus an enlightened Metro council.

Today, as we face the first proposed property tax increase in six years, I, like most of you, have no fondness for paying more taxes. Yet, I also know that to keep our vital city moving forward and addressing our growing needs and our opportunity for potential greatness, we must invest in our future. Frankly, I'm impressed and amazed at the job Mayor Karl Dean and his team has done in keeping the momentum going during one of the toughest economic times which our country has endured since the Great Depression of the 1930s. They have stayed on task, on course and on target with the priorities of education, public safety and economic development. And, now, it is time for Metro property owners to step up even if it means doing so with reluctance and gritted teeth.

If one thinks about it, we have a lot of "sugar" here:

- Lowest taxes of any of Tennessee's largest cities
- A brightening economic outlook, and
- Competent and focused governmental leadership

Like any medicine, tax increases are not necessarily savored. However, a prescription of a bit of seemingly distasteful but preventative medicine allows us to remain healthy. I encourage everyone to study this issue and develop an informed opinion with the strains of "A Spoonful of Sugar" echoing faintly in the background.

DEMOCRATS PLAYING LETHAL GAME WITH GUNS

MAY 7, 2012

DEMOCRATS PLAYING LETHAL GAME WITH GUNS
By Bo Roberts

As this final (allegedly) legislative week unfolds, my fellow Democrats (the remaining few left in the General Assembly) brought shame to our party.

Playing political games can be entertaining, but to play games with guns is no laughing or recreational matter. The overall story is the battle over guns in parking lots. Tennessee has been thrust into the spotlight with that issue when the attention should be focused on the budget and wrapping up this session in a responsible fashion.

Responsibility is something the Democrats abandoned when, on the Senate floor and in the House Calendar and Rules committee, they attempted to force the Republicans to vote on bringing the issue to the floor for a vote. While I understand the strategy, I, along with many others, are dismayed that this particular issue was the one selected for use in a game of one-upmanship.

College football coach Steve Spurrier turned his "fun and gun" offense into quite a success at the University of Florida, but he was using young adults who were simply playing a game,

103

not fully mature Americans dealing with the finality of life and death.

The blame, which can be ascribed to all Democrats who went along, is squarely centered on the leadership: Sen. Jim Kyle in the senate and Rep. Mike Turner in the house. How can these party leaders expect us to receive R-E-S-P-E-C-T when we are not RESPONSIBLE? I think the only way we can regain stature is to resist those in the legislature who are the thorns in the side of responsible Republicans and reasonable Tennesseans everywhere.

Tennessee businesses, education leaders, and law enforcement officials all oppose this bill. Surely they must be shocked at the power of the National Rifle Association and their cohorts.

Watching the blatant bullying by the NRA, it would not be surprising to see the barrel of this ugly issue raised again before the session ends. If, and when it does, I hope my fellow Democrats will stop playing with gunfire and do the right thing. Just ask your friends associated with Virginia Tech whether they are still suffering from the tragedy that occurred there. They can certainly attest to the fact that this is very serious business, indeed.

WE NEED MORE PURPLE, LESS RED AND BLUE

NOVEMBER 30, 2012

WE NEED MORE PURPLE, LESS RED AND BLUE
By Bo Roberts

As I was contemplating writing a column pleading for more mature and measured bipartisan efforts in the face of our nation's presumed forthcoming fiscal disaster, I recalled the column I wrote exactly four years ago about a "purple coalition" and what the Volunteer State could offer America's new president early on in his administration.

Though my support for President Barack Obama was less enthusiastic during the 2012 election cycle than it was in 2008, I still believe that what he offered and stood for was, ultimately, the better choice on the most recent Election Day. I'm not sure, though, that we can survive if we continue with the vitriolic political approach that has stagnated and stained our great country during the past two years. In retrospect, I don't think that I can actually offer any better advice than I did four years ago. The following column was printed in The Tennessean in January 2009:

When almost 30 Nashvillians gathered at our house last month, we had at least three things in common:

- We were all supporters of President-elect Barack Obama.
- Not one of us was a Davidson County native.

- We each hoped for an inclusive administration seeking bipartisan solutions to the monumental challenges now facing America.

As one of the more than 4,500 "Obama house parties" held throughout the nation during the second weekend in December, our group was impressively diverse: multiracial, multiparty and multigenerational, from teachers to investment bankers to the recently unemployed. Our "charge" was to gather input for the Obama transition team.

It was an enlightening, inspirational two hours on a cold, gray Saturday afternoon.

We themed the event "A Blue County in a Red State," since Davidson was just one of four Tennessee counties that gave Obama a majority. Reflecting later, I thought about the group's common desire for bipartisan solutions and realized that the Volunteer State had much to offer the president-elect and his team. Listening closely and broadly would be their first task.

Consider creating a "Color Purple" coalition and include the congressmen from two of the "bluest" counties, the brilliant Jim Cooper from Nashville and the enigmatic, energetic Steve Cohen from Memphis. I could see them teaming with two "red" representatives with extensive and successful stints in local and state government in Tennessee: Sens.

Lamar Alexander (a former two-term governor) and Bob Corker (former Chattanooga mayor and former state finance commissioner).

The blue mix from the U.S. House of Representatives would acknowledge the early campaign loyalty of Cooper and Cohen, who represent Tennessee's largest metropolitan areas and are fully aware of the recession-laden suffering of an urban area.

The "red" mix from the U.S. Senate offers two men who surmounted challenges as chief executive officers of their state and city, respectively. Both senators concluded their terms with a long list of accomplishments, high approval ratings and track records of reaching "across the aisle" to solve problems and meet challenges. Their voices are those who understand the complex realities of what works best at those governmental levels. Their hands-on experiences could prove invaluable in crafting a bipartisan stimulus plan.

The current issues that our country is facing are neither red nor blue; they are, however, dauntingly colorblind. Like the other Middle Tennesseans gathered in our living room, I am inspired by President Obama's transformational message of hope, his reservoir of intelligence and his calm, yet firm sense of courage. His has clearly pointed out that he can't do it alone; he wants and needs our helping hands.

Part of our collective suggestion is that he consider the highly qualified, down-home input that a purple-colored coalition would provide. God bless you for hearing our voices, Mr. President. Please keep listening.

THE CASE FOR SPORTS (AND A DOMED STADIUM) FOR NASHVILLE

MARCH 25, 2013

(When this column was published more than 10 years ago, I was chided by many friends, and scorned by enemies, for proposing such a preposterous idea. In May of 2023 Metro Council completed approvals for a $2.1 billion dollar plan for a new domed stadium and a revamped downtown East Nashville plan, which I fully supported in my March 2023 column)

THE CASE FOR SPORTS (AND A DOMED STADIUM) FOR NASHVILLE

By Bo Roberts

When NashvilleNext, the community-driven process for guiding Metro Nashville through 2040 recently began pondering what we should look like as a city 27 years from now, one indelible image came to mind: a climate-controlled football stadium. Our own Music City Dome?

First, let me document precisely how sports have broadened Nashville's appeal and the profound impact which sporting events have had in elevating Nashville to its freshly anointed "It" city status. Having been a resident here since 1985 and an active participant in Music City's business, civic and sports communities, I feel qualified to offer an opinion.

It all began more than 20 years ago when then-mayor and sports enthusiast Dick Fulton formally organized the Nashville Sports Council (NSC), which celebrates two decades in existence on March 7 with its Pepsi Celebration of Champions presented by Kroger. When the awards celebration convenes at the Grand Ole Opry next week to announce its 2012 winners, attendees will also enjoy an all-encompassing salute to the top 20 sports events staged here since 1993. (Tickets are available at the door or contact ebest@nashvillesports.com).

Arena the Catalyst

During those years, a mayor who was not the least bit sports-oriented imagined a new arena as the single most vital element in the redevelopment of Nashville's downtown district. Then-mayor Phil Bredesen's far-reaching vision that such a facility would serve as the crucial driving economic development force to spur downtown redevelopment was right on target. As part of the arena development plan, the Country Music Hall of Fame moved to the area now known as SoBro, followed by a host of other economic "drivers" including the Hilton hotel, The Palm restaurant, the Schermerhorn Symphony Center and on and on.

Those of you who lived in Nashville in the '90s might recall the bleak state of lower Broadway, populated as it was then primarily by a surfeit of x-rated businesses while pausing now to marvel at the incredible amount of territory we've covered in the intervening years.

It was a real breakthrough when the Nashville Predators arrived in 1998 as the anchor tenant for the city's new, architecturally imposing arena. A year later, the Houston Oilers came a'callin'. Mayor Bredesen, scorched by an earlier flirtation with the New Jersey Devils management when they parlayed their far-fetched move to Nashville into construction of a new arena there instead, said he would only proceed with an "exclusive right to negotiate." We all know the outcome of that decision: a stadium referendum vote with a resounding 60% of the vote. Do you remember Nashville without the Titans? While they may be struggling on the field a bit now, sold-out throngs continue to make their way to LP Field for NFL football.

Runners, Bowl Games and More

Another major sporting event created and developed during this period was the now- nationally recognized Country Music Marathon and Half-Marathon. What would April be in Nashville without the more than 30,000 fleet-footed athletes descending here to pound the streets in this highly popular, music-accented race?

Following the stadium's completion, the far-sighted folks at the Sports Council decided to pursue and develop a bowl game. And, presto, the Music City Bowl was born in 1998, and a separate corporation (same staff) formed. The ultimate impact of holding those contests during what is usually the year's slowest tourism week; quite significant, I'd say. The bowl has transcended into one of the top non-BCS level games, often leading the pack in three key rankings: out of town visitors, television ratings and economic impact (over $214 million and counting).

The NSC has also presented four college football games at the stadium with a fifth coming this fall: the season-opener between Western Kentucky and Kentucky, a match–up featuring the debut of both teams' new head coaches.

The return of the SEC men's basketball tournament here this month kicks-off a three-out-of-four year stay for that tournament, interrupted only by the 2014 Women's Final Four, while marking the NSC's 29th postseason basketball event. We enjoyed several notable NCAA March Madness events as part of that count, too. Additionally, the organization has recruited national figure skating and gymnastic events for Nashville, generating a total economic impact exceeding $100 million. The more one tracks the numbers the more mind-boggling they seem.

Sports Industry a Player

Is all this to say that sports are the single most important activity which have occurred in Nashville during the past 20 years? No, but a compelling, definitive case can be made regarding the relevance of sports and world-class facilities. Obviously, they're a solidly undeniable economic factor for the region, and surely represent one of the lifestyle components influencing Nashville's designation as one of America's hottest cities.

The NashvilleNext folks should certainly consider drafting and wholeheartedly embracing sports as one of the main centerpieces of their exciting envisioning plan. The major economic impact and the lifestyle enhancements for thousands of residents and visitors are simply undeniable. Readers should note that the impact figures cited here only reflect the directly sponsored NSC events. We haven't even begun to account for the additional millions (billions?) more collectively generated by the Predators, Titans, and area colleges or the astounding revenue numbers which the arena's music events can claim.

Sporting events in downtown Nashville are now spectacularly successful because our ever-changing downtown "campus," with its multitude of hotels, restaurants and entertainment offerings, is enticing fans from across the nation to visit Music City. Though they may be initially drawn by the sports activities, there's no question that the fans also patronize the city's other attractions during their stays. The outstanding effort led by the Nashville CVB to brand us as "Music City," with all that our unique music industry provides, undoubtedly sets us apart from every other city anywhere in the world.

Buoyed by these extraordinary successes, what should a dynamic, thriving sports landscape look like in the mid-state a quarter of a century from now?

First, I believe there will eventually be a new, first-class baseball stadium downtown, and, secondly and more long-term, a climate-controlled, domed stadium, as well. Such a facility would bring a plethora of possibilities: an SEC championship football game, a national college championship football game and, hold onto your seat licenses, friends—yes, even a Super Bowl. To this one could add the Music City Bowl competing for ongoing national semi-finals games, winter and spring soccer matches without weather concerns, the NCAA Men's Final Four and...well, toss the imagination ball as high and wide as you can.

Regardless, I'm certain that there'll be plenty to cheer about.

The economic payoffs would be enormous not to mention the additional lifestyle choices, which would be pretty cool, too. Let's think BIG, Nashville. Based on where we were not too long ago, it seems that thinking big no longer means "just dreaming" big.

WHITE PEOPLE WELCOME, TOO: NO EXCEPTIONS

MARCH 26, 2013

WHITE PEOPLE WELCOME, TOO: NO EXCEPTIONS
By Bo Roberts

"Is this the biggest crowd of white people you've ever had in your church?"

That question was asked of Rev. Ed Sanders during a funeral visitation for a close friend (who happened to have been an African-American who counted scores of Caucasians among his legions of intimates).

"Not at all," the charismatic pastor of Nashville's inclusive Metropolitan Interdenominational Church replied as he explained what he meant. During the funeral service the following day, Reverend Sanders took the opportunity to mention the question to the more than 400 gathered there, most of whom had entered the church for the first time that morning.

When he revealed to the mourners that the greatest number of whites ever assembled in his house of worship was at the funeral of James Earl Ray in 1998. As this was startling information for most in the congregation, one could almost hear the whirring of hundreds of minds processing and reconciling this surprising fact: they were sitting in the one place willing to hold a service for the murderer of esteemed civil rights leader Martin Luther King, Jr.

Following Ray's death in prison more than 30 years after King's assassination, his family turned to noted nonviolent activist James Lawson of Nashville, who had ministered to Ray. Upon receiving a call from Lawson, Rev. Sanders quickly agreed to conduct the funeral at the church he had founded in north Nashville in 1981. Ray's service, which attracted international media attention, also drew among those present, many infamous White Supremacists, who attended, allegedly, with expectations of a "damming to hell" rather than the dignified proceeding that transpired.

As Rev. Sanders related this riveting story to us a few months ago, he directed our attention to a sign in the sanctuary proclaiming the church's creed: "...A community of believers, inclusive of all and alienating to none."

He said in a voice that fellow pallbearer and former Nashville mayor Bill Purcell described as "what God must sound like" that inclusion didn't mean "we welcome all EXCEPT ...we don't say we are tolerant of all EXCEPT...or that God loves everyone EXCEPT...it just doesn't, or shouldn't work that way."

The audience on that day, brought together to celebrate departed friend Emmett Edwards, was as eclectic and wide-ranging as Emmett's life. He was your friend regardless of color, gender, religion, sexual orientation, income level, or even political persuasion (though a lifelong, die-hard Democrat, the sight of his Republican friends in the crowd would have pleased him).

Rev. Sanders' remarks resonated in my mind last week as I circulated among the diverse crowd of 900 at the Tennessee State Museum for a viewing of the original Emancipation Proclamation from the National Archives in Washington. As I stood surveying the eclectic crowd, I pondered how many there had ever been cast into the "except" category while I yearned to hear the searing stories they could tell about the Proclamation's impact...lo' these many years later.

Much like the creed of Rev. Sander's church, the document, though written on 150-year-old fragile, light-sensitive paper, contained just simple words. Yet, on that evening at that momentous occasion—they were the most extraordinary, most powerful, most compelling words anywhere.

DICK BARRY: PART OF THE TENNESSEE HISTORY HE LOVED

JULY 15, 2013

DICK BARRY: PART OF THE TENNESSEE HISTORY HE LOVED
By Bo Roberts

Grey was the overwhelming, predominant hair color amidst the mostly male crowd gathered recently to celebrate the life of our mutual, just-departed friend, William L. (Dick) Barry of Lexington, TN.

Appropriately, we congregated in the House of Representatives chamber, where Dick served two distinguished terms as Speaker (1961-65). We all sat captivated by Dick's commanding voice as an audiotape of his first acceptance speech echoed throughout the hallowed hall. Serving as emcee of the occasion was Republican lawmaker Rep. Steve McDaniel of Lexington, who had a special relationship with his Democratic predecessor. They had a friendship based on respect (Steve was the first Republican Dick ever voted for), a love of history and a passion for the Volunteer State.

The group was enthralled with the recollections about Dick's quiet influence from Judges Frank Clement and William Koch and moved by the eloquence of former governor Winfield Dunn and Anne Wagner, daughter of former governor Buford Ellington, as they honored this elder statesman prior to Sen.

Douglas Henry's powerful and fitting delivery of the legislature's joint resolution.

Enthusiasm for history was the binding force for many in this particular audience, as most in the room were themselves a force in shaping Tennessee's political history.

Following Dick's tenure in the legislature, he served as an assistant attorney general, but it was his service in the government's executive branch where I felt privileged to work beside him. As legal counsel, Dick handled the legislative side of things on Gov. Ellington's staff while I looked after the departments and administrative side. As a youngster/newcomer to that level of government, I benefited immensely from Dick's solid, subtle mentorship while he delighted in noting that, in four years as colleagues, we never had a cross word.

Shortly after Ellington's term concluded, though, Dick orchestrated what is still considered one of most significant "coups" ever in Tennessee governmental history. Prior to the inauguration of Governor-elect Dunn (the first Republican governor in 50 years), the majority legislative party held its Democratic caucus nomination for constitutional officers. To the surprise of many, fresh political operative Floyd Kephart (running on a more partisan, more political platform) won the comptroller nomination, seemingly ousting legendary veteran Bill Snodgrass.

But, behind-the-scenes Dick moved swiftly to counsel with like-minded Democrats and Republicans to create a progressive coalition to overturn the caucus vote and re-elect Snodgrass. While a shock to the political system, Dick's triumph kept our state from straying from its well-honed, strong, honest approach to government. It's not coincidental that Snodgrass' name is today chiseled on the state's imposing Tennessee Tower.

And, that was just one instance where Dick Barry demonstrated his reverence for history while acting to change how it'd be written in the future. Respect was the currency Dick dealt in and he gave as good as he got. His actions then should serve as a potent reminder for all current office holders, lest they forget that our hair wasn't grey back then either.

MAJOR SHIFTS UNDERWAY IN THE WAY TENNESSEE EDUCATION AND GOVERNMENT OPERATE

AUGUST 23, 2013

MAJOR SHIFTS UNDERWAY IN THE WAY TENNESSEE EDUCATION AND GOVERNMENT OPERATE

By Bo Roberts

"Some people have 15 years of experience; some have one year's experience 15 times."

That's a maxim which I learned decades ago, which accurately reflects the paradigm shift taking place in the way Tennessee state government and our public education system now operates.

Laws have already gone into effect this summer radically altering the state's half-century old Civil Service system. In education, it's the revamped compensation plan for our public school teachers.

I know many of my fellow Democrats are strongly resisting these changes, but I believe they are holding onto outdated modes of thinking. Changes needed to occur. Our energy and efforts should be directed to ensuring that the new direction is now applied as fairly and effectively as possible.

There are some significant points that those implementing the changes should keep in mind:

121

There are thousands of smart, dedicated, service-oriented state employees and educators who have served the Volunteer State with enthusiasm and aplomb for many years;

Tennessee state government has long been recognized as one of the best-run states in the nation; and Many top and mid-level managers will have to make serious changes themselves.

With regard to the last point, envision that managers may be required to interview in-house applicants whose qualifications are occasionally overshadowed by their looming level of seniority. Dismissing a Civil Service-protected employee can take as much as two years unless there are major violations. Further, when funds were available for pay increases in the past, these were essentially applied equally, across the board, with no regard for outstanding or exceptional performance.

For managers unaccustomed to actively overseeing every aspect of their departments it is a completely new day. How those managers react to this sweeping cultural change will also eventually determine whether or not they themselves are right for their jobs.

At the same time, the top managers (department heads) in Gov. Bill Haslam's administration should begin their evaluations from a place of respect. They should honor the fact that while there may be problems, state government has existed long before the current folks arrived and will be there long after they depart. They should also carefully try to discern which specific employees actually have the appropriate and necessary skills to make positive contributions to "the customer's" experience—-i.e., those they are reportedly serving: the stakeholders/taxpayers, who are the citizens of Tennessee.

For our educators, the exceptional ones should have no worries. It's worthwhile that experience and advanced degrees are still a part of the equation, but the key shift is the inclusion of documentable results, which, as I understand it, are based on test score performance. Hopefully the test score process can be balanced to accommodate such things as income inequality as well as language barriers. Here, too, those administrators making the call should begin with respect while treading lightly during the challenging days ahead.

To those who contend that Tennessee's government should be run "like a business," I believe instead the state should serve its citizens in a professional, "businesslike" manner.

AMP IS A START FOR CITY THAT NEEDS MASS TRANSIT

(The first actual vote to initiate a rapid transit system was defeated by a substantial margin on this effort; the next attempt came in 2018, a proposal for a more widespread and costly combination of transit solutions that also lost by a substantial margin. The quest for transit solutions continues as the population and traffic increases).

AMP IS A START FOR CITY THAT NEEDS MASS TRANSIT
By Bo Roberts

Have you ever pondered the origin of the term "doubleheader"?

Surprisingly, it was hatched in reference to a transit need. During the late 19th century, as New York City baseball teams began scheduling two games for the price of a single admission on the same day, train operators coined the phrase. Why? Because they had to add a second engine (header) to pull the extra cars anticipated for the larger-than-normal crowds. Later, "doubleheader" became a description for a baseball event before morphing into a catchall expression describing any kind of two-event day.

But, you might ask, what does that have to do with Nashville's proposed Amp project?

Soon after the Titans began playing at LP Field, I decided to forgo my season parking pass and take advantage of mass transit. That wise decision enabled me to leave home at 11:10 a.m., park at Greer Stadium, hop on a fast-moving bus using dedicated lanes and be seated and enjoying a Logan's cheeseburger before the noon kickoff. After the game, I could be home by 4 p.m.

These disparate examples illustrate moving people in different, yet convenient ways. Mass-transit "magic" at work.

So, can we demonstrate a demand that justifies the cost and temporary inconveniences of the proposed Amp? In a word: yes. The necessity already exists and will only grow as our increasingly attractive region becomes even more popular.

When I hear folks complaining about Nashville's traffic issues, I think: Compared with what? Perhaps they've never experienced Atlanta's world-famous rush hour. Or maybe they've never known any of the prepared-with-a-book Tampa-St. Petersburg residents who rarely cross the Bay bridge without reading material to help endure the notorious wait. Fortunately, we're not there yet. But we're headed in that potentially disastrous direction. Taking proactive steps now to create more efficient, effective ways of moving citizens throughout and around Music City simply makes sense.

I have many good friends who live in the West End corridor (as I do) who are actively and adamantly opposed to the Amp. I respect their opinions because I don't believe they're categorically opposed to change of any kind. I know change for change's sake is not necessarily the answer. However, I also know that times and traffic density here have surpassed easy resolution. I've heard people declare that Nashville is becoming

"another Atlanta," which I consider a concern rather than an aspiration. Our hopes are that we (the region) are smart enough to make mostly correct choices as we address ways to maintain a lifestyle that makes us so appealing to newcomers.

Is the Amp a cure-all for our future challenges? Certainly not. However, it's a start, a step toward shaping the somewhat unknowable without waiting to be constrained by the inevitable. Is the Amp the perfect first step? As there are few "perfect" approaches, I'm confident that the much-maligned Amp plan will undergo some adjustments before any possible implementation. Keep in mind that less than 20 years ago, we had no inkling that getting to an NFL game would be cause for any real consideration. Because, after all, having an NFL team in Nashville was absolutely inconceivable ... right?

I think, and hope, that the Amp gets us ready for our forthcoming doubleheader, whatever form it may take.

HIGHER EDUCATION CUTS HURT FAMILIES

JUNE 2, 2014

HIGHER EDUCATION CUTS HURT FAMILIES
By Bo Roberts

To most of us, $19 million is a whole lot of money; it's certainly much more than the oft-referenced cost of a cup of coffee.

But, that's the specific amount sliced from Tennessee's allocation to public higher education institutions for the fiscal year beginning on July 1. While the governor was forced to reduce his entire budget after a lackluster year in tax revenue collections, $19 million represented a huge number, both literally and psychologically, to college and university administrators throughout the state. They had "earned" that money by excelling at a new system designed to reward productivity. Student enrollment numbers were no longer the ultimate benchmark.

So, just how much is $19 million in the grand budgetary scheme of things? It's a mere hundredth of 1 percent of the overall $12.7 billion state budget. To put that in perspective, a family with a gross annual income of $100,000 would have to adjust its budget by $150. At approximately one cup of coffee a week, though, most wouldn't call that a threat to making their mortgage payment.

We all understand that budget choices are agonizing. We've been there. Yet it comes down to plain priorities: public higher

education has been suffering from a lack of preferential treatment for decades.

I say this while acknowledging that Gov. Bill Haslam has
put more emphasis and given more attention to our colleges
and universities than any other governor in recent memory. In
fact, the budget reduction cited here was made to one of this
administration's strongest new initiatives: an effort to alter the
culture of higher education by focusing on results (graduates)
rather than enrollment totals. Haslam's bold approach, coupled
with his "Drive for 55" to increase the number of college graduates in the Volunteer State, and his "Tennessee Promise" to
make tuition free to community colleges and colleges of applied
technology, is indicative of the allegiance this administration
has devoted to this particular issue.

However, don't miss the fact that the governor is battling
a funding trend that began many administrations ago. Here's
a tale-telling snapshot of recent history: 20 years ago, tuition
covered about one-third of the revenues for public higher
education; 10 years later, tuition costs had doubled and the
amount students paid was up to 50 percent of the revenues.
Today, tuition has quadrupled and covers nearly two-thirds
of revenues. As any tuition-paying parent in Tennessee would
agree, it's far more than a casual cup of coffee.

How did this happen? Choices. When crunch time came, it
seemed fairly painless for administrations and legislators to

resist covering increasing education costs because they fully understood that the institutions could make those costs up by simply increasing tuition. The misery was passed along, so to speak, alleviating any potential hue and cry from the voters about "raising taxes."

Speaking of suffering, Gov. Haslam was recently quoted as saying "nothing pained him more" than the cuts he had to make to raises for teachers, state employees and to higher education. We can commiserate with him because it has truly been a time of tough decisions.

But, back to choices. My hope is that when the choices are made during the next legislative session, a "cup of coffee" for higher education will take precedence over other, seemingly more important priorities. It should make the final cut. We'll take the coffee plain, please, no cappuccinos or frills needed.

METRO SCHOOL BOARD: DO YOU REALLY BELIEVE ANYONE WANTS TO WORK FOR YOU?

SEPTEMBER 28, 2015

**METRO SCHOOL BOARD: DO YOU REALLY BELIEVE
ANYONE WANTS TO WORK FOR YOU?**

By Bo Roberts

A message to Metro School Board members: To coin a phrase from that highly regarded 20th century philosopher Groucho Marx, "I wouldn't hire someone who would come to work for me."

Groucho's reference was to not belonging to a club that would have him as a member. His words came instantly to mind while assessing the Board's dysfunctional operations during the past couple of years. I think you made a good move at your retreat (BTW is that a noun or a verb?) in forming a community group to seek the best candidates. Such an effort will bring some impressive candidates to the forefront. However, I don't think that it will lead to any constructive results if the Board continues to function using its recent behavior patterns.

Two illustrations:

When Karl Dean was elected mayor eight years ago, he jumped quickly into the process of preparing his office to take over education in an effort to develop local leadership in anticipation of the state's takeover. Shortly after that, the Board hired a "compromise" candidate. Jesse Register quickly settled things down and got the focus on the students of

Davidson County. It was a shot of confidence to state and local officials. Supt. Register did an outstanding job by any measurement. I can only imagine how relieved he was to exit such a contentious situation having worked with such an ineffective Board.

Secondly, when the Board selected Dr. Mike Looney, it seemed MPNS lucked up and hit a home run. Dr. Looney, having dealt with a somewhat dysfunctional board himself, had seen his community come together. People realized that it wasn't fun and games; they were dealing with the lives of children, and then begged him to stay. Surveying Nashville's education leadership, who could blame Looney for saying "no thanks." Williamson County should send the Metro School Board a thank you note.

Ladies and gentlemen of the board, you are all good people. But at some point you must realize that the fearful, yet wide-eyed expectant children entering our schools for the first time, after leaving the cocoon of their parents' support, trust that they are arriving in a safe learning harbor.

That trust is more important than any philosophy or ideology that any one person holds. You now have an excellent opportunity to establish a new bond with our bright and energetic mayor, Megan Barry.

Our community, our mayor, and our children all deserve better. Nashville is an attractive place for professionals to work. But, I can only wonder if anyone with talent wants to take the job you have to offer knowing that an inordinate amount of valuable energy will be devoted to dealing with a divided Board?

Please, please, take a look in the mirror. Find a way to achieve consensus. Do what's best for our students. Override your political, bureaucratic, and ideological issues. We need you. Now.

THE LAST STRAW?

NOVEMBER 10, 2016

(After attending my first business meeting following recovery from brain surgery, I was tired from staying up late watching the disastrous 2016 presidential election. I went to my office immediately after to write this column, the first of many (some trying to take a hopeful slant) that mentioned Donald Trump.)

THE LAST STRAW?

By Bo Roberts

Was Donald Trump's election victory America's "last straw?"

The idiom "last straw" comes from the 19th century English proverb:

"The final straw that broke the camel's back." My answer: I think not.

While as many as half of American voters feared this astounding upset, I don't believe that we have quite reached our limits. Look at how many "last straws" Trump had in the past year and a half. Each time he personally attacked one of his primary opponents (Little Rubio, Crazy Cruz and on and on), the national media pundits said that might be the straw that broke the proverbial primary camel's back.

Then when he brow-beat and bullied all of his opponents to win the primary, the straws of the general election began piling up. From ridiculing a disabled reporter, to insulting a Miss Universe pageant winner, to calling our U.S. military a disaster, to insulting a Gold Star family and a judge because his parents were of Mexican heritage, to calling Sen. John McCain a coward.... It seemed, like we waited daily for the debut of each new "Trumpism." Most any one of those could have been considered the "last straw."

The repetitive "straws" seemed to numb both the populace and the media. Ah, but then, came the infamous "locker room" tapes......surely that would be the last straw? Um, guess not.

My take is that when people are mad they have passion, and there are obviously millions of very unhappy folks out there and Trump knew just how to fire them up. While they might not actually know what they were mad about, whatever it was, people seemed to feel that Trump must be with them because everyone was mad at him, so, obviously, he's with the collective us. It didn't matter "what" he said, the angry supporters liked the "way" he was saying it. My take is that anger generates passionate ire which in turn generates action. The "action" translated into votes. It happened in the primary with the most GOP votes in history.....clearly there were newly energized voters for Trump.

Plus, it was the biggest wipeout of "general wisdom" that I have ever witnessed. I and many others thought that Trump would flame out no later than October 2015. Looking back one could watch any presidential news segment and Trump's name would come up as many times as all of the primary candidates and was used four times to any one time use of Ms. Clinton's name in the general election.

General wisdom (yep, me too) said Ms. Clinton was much more qualified, would turn out the coalition of minority groups (all labeled with derisive insults by The Donald), and that things would then settle down. Most every Republican I am acquainted with said they simply could not vote for The Donald.

Yet "general wisdom" didn't account for passion and action on the other side. Other than the Hispanic vote (generated mostly against Mr. Trump), Hillary simply didn't generate the kind of devoted passion or excitement that turned into votes cast.

Even though the president-elect tossed out enough straws to cripple a platoon, I think we will survive. For more than 240 years, our nation has survived wars almost from its infancy, including one four-year bloodbath against ourselves (the devastating Civil War); many scandals, as well as multiple crippling depressions. Yes, many foundation-shaking straws have been tossed on America's back. Not only have we survived, we have prospered and become the richest, strongest and finest nation on earth.

We can and will survive the Trump straw. But, now's the time, Mr. President-elect, for resting the straw tossing for just a bit.

HOW SEN. HENRY MADE ME A POLITICAL HYPOCRITE

MARCH 8, 2017

(Sen. Douglas Selph Henry died on March 3, 2017 not long after retiring as the longest serving member of the state legislature in Tennessee history. Leigh and I were fortunate to spend some time with him just a few days before he died. A legislative icon who embodied the role of public servant, he would have added the qualifier "gentleman" to the phrase. Like many, I often disagreed with him but unwaveringly supported his integrity and wisdom.

This column was written two weeks before he died then published later in the GCA News).

HOW SEN. HENRY MADE ME A POLITICAL HYPOCRITE
By Bo Roberts

It was a sweltering August day seven summers ago when my loyalty and allegiance to esteemed state Sen. Douglas Henry (a friend of four decades and a marvelous mentor to many), momentarily turned me from a person of steadfast conviction into a bit of a political hypocrite.

This story actually began in early 2009 when I made an appointment to meet with then-Mayor Bill Haslam of Knoxville to encourage him to consider a run for governor in 2010. Because his dad and I, "Big Jim" Haslam, had known each other and worked together on many bi-partisan community efforts over the years, I took a keen interest in seeing Bill's political career evolve. I was impressed with the job that he had done as mayor, and as we got to know each other, came to appreciate his vision, intelligence and integrity.

He said he was considering it, though he did have several significant projects in Knoxville that he wanted to see to fruition. I believed that Bill would be the best person to be our next governor long before any others had announced their intentions and encouraged him to give the idea more serious consideration. I was pleased when he decided to move forward, though I knew our meeting didn't really impact his final decision.

After consulting with Bill's top advisors (Tom Ingram and campaign manager Mark Cate), I invited two dozen Democratic friends to meet Bill that February. As a volunteer in the campaign, I encouraged my Democratic friends to vote in the Republican primary to ensure that candidate Haslam ultimately became the nominee...many of us felt it was crucial to the future of our state.

However, as primary voting day loomed, I was receiving unsettling reports that my friend Doug had an unusually serious primary challenge on his hands. As I crossed the street from my home to cast my vote at West End Middle School, I was genuinely torn between which primary to choose. At the last minute, I became a hypocrite and voted in the

Democratic primary. I knew then that I had to support my hero, Sen. Henry, in the final race of his political career. I told no one about my decision.

Later that night I attended the Haslam election event in downtown Nashville, where the victory came early. I then headed to Sen. Henry's Green Hills headquarters, arriving just as the final results were announced: He won by a single vote. (A recount would swell the good Senator's final margin to 17 votes. Of course, we didn't know that then).

That momentous evening will be forever etched in my mind. The joyous celebration had concluded and almost everyone had departed when Sen. Henry's trusted colleague asked if I would walk him to his car. During our brief journey, he said: "Well, Bo, I guess one vote is as good as a thousand," an assessment with which I heartily concurred. He noted that he was going home "to kiss Miss Lolly, have a glass of whiskey and a cigar and sit on my front porch and relax a bit." He explained that he never imbibed before completing all of his obligations.

Several times following Sen. Henry's retirement four years later, we shared a glass of whiskey together on that very porch, as we mulled the issues of the day. My final visit with him was Thursday evening before he passed away. I shared with him my three-word summation that I had been thinking about all afternoon: I told him he was "Tennessee's Best Friend."

He loved the Volunteer State unconditionally, without hesitation or reservation. And, his state returned that admiration wholeheartedly.

I believe that Gov. Haslam, knowing how much he, too, came to respect Sen. Doug Henry, will forgive me for my one political transgression.

HEALTH CARE: IS EXPECTING REASON UNREASONABLE?

JULY 12, 2017

HEALTH CARE: IS EXPECTING REASON UNREASONABLE?
By Bo Roberts

I couldn't tell if it was an admonition or a threat when Republican Senate Majority Leader Mitch McConnell told his GOP cohorts that if they didn't pass some version of the health care bill, they would...... OMG!.....have to work with the Democrats to reach a solution.

For some perspective, let's not lose sight of the fact that eight years ago, Democrats passed what became known as "Obamacare" without a single Republican vote. Speaker Nancy Pelosi led the charge then with her "we have the votes, thus the power, we don't need them" approach.

Is it too much to ask that reasonable men and women from each party actually get together and create a plan that might address our nation's health care needs?

To do so, the yapping from both the far right and far left will need to fall on the deaf ears of those trying to actually work something out. It's hard to forget seven years of GOP rhetoric claiming that the repeal of Obamacare could solve all of the nation's problems, particularly when it came from the same group which has devoted zero time to devising a plan that is superior, or that might actually pass.

The many Democratic members who wouldn't defend the Affordable Care Act nor make any notable attempt to correct its flaws are not without blame.

Even the current president has continued to reiterate that Obamacare will be repealed and replaced with "something better, much much better." Now he's saying, "hey, I need another checkmark....let's repeal now and replace later."

There is evidence, however, that the process can actually work in

Washington, D.C. To wit, the efforts of Tennessee's own Senator Lamar Alexander: his committee crafted a bilateral rewrite and simplified direction for our nation's education system, and then did the same for an overhaul and greater investment in medical research by the National Institute of Health.

Frankly, I was hopeful when the battle shifted to the Senate, that Sen. Alexander could lead and formulate a reasonable and effective piece of legislation. Alas, I'm not sure what happened when Leader McConnell decided to bypass the committee system and set up a committee of 13 white men to carve out a cure. Yes, I am aware that Sen. Alexander was one of that number, but one of 13 is just that....not the chair of a committee which is supposed to be addressing this crucial issue.

It's way above my pay grade to offer any specific or technical solutions. But, I do not think it is above the pay grade of what I hope is an actual majority of Americans who want things to actually work within the Beltway. Maybe, just maybe, if each member of Congress could change the conversation from WBFMP (What's best for my party) to WBFOC (What's best for our country), we could actually replace the zeal to repeal with a road to reason.

I realize that is a quixotic aspiration, though maybe not for a coalition of reasonable individuals stitched together in an effort to actually solve something. Surely, it's worth a try.

82 WORLD'S FAIR MAY HOLD LESSON FOR TRUMP AND NORTH KOREA

JUNE 21, 2018

82 WORLD'S FAIR MAY HOLD LESSON
FOR TRUMP AND NORTH KOREA
By Bo Roberts

Maybe, just maybe (based on a personal experience years ago), there might be some hope in President Donald Trump's recent meeting with Kim Jong Un, North Korea's leader.

As one who detests the performance of just about anything Trump does, and yet as an American, I truly hope this venture is successful beyond the momentous photo opportunity it provided for both participants.

My aspirations stem from my unanticipated venture into international events starting in 1980 when President Jimmy Carter announced that the U.S. would boycott the Summer Olympics slated for Moscow later that year. I was CEO of the 1982 World's Fair in Knoxville, and the Soviet Union was already constructing what was projected to be the largest (and anchor) exhibit at our event. Soon after Carter's announcement in March, however, we were informed that the "Russians weren't coming."

We immediately pivoted our efforts to the People's Republic of China, which had never participated in a World's Fair. Following many visits and after calling in every possible political favor, we recruited China, which became by far the most popular pavilion at the fair. However, the reason for my hope now stems from my first visit to China in 1980.

Want to submit your letter to the editor? Here is how. Wochit I was hosted by their government, which was just over a decade removed from that nation's devastating "Cultural Revolution," which essentially deprived an entire generation from being educated while shutting them off from the world.

I noticed as I was being driven into town from the Beijing airport that the main thoroughfare was crowded with masses of bicycles, more than 80 percent bicycles, the primary mode of transportation, and that almost everyone was dressed in either blue or olive green "Mao" suits.

FILE – *In this Feb. 5, 1972 file photo, U.S. President Richard Nixon shakes hands with Communist leader Mao Tze-tung during Nixon's historic trip to Communist China.*

The two countries had no relations whatsoever from 1949, when Mao Zedong's communists took power, to 1979, when Jimmy Carter and Deng Xiaoping established diplomatic ties that have endured through good times and tension ever since. The relationship is usually cordial, but the long game is one of unease: China has long believed the United States is trying to contain it, and Washington views Beijing's economic heft and increasing presence on the world stage as a strategic and economic threat.

On my first night there, my hosts took me on a tour of China's capital city, proudly pointing out certain restaurants where U.S. President Richard Nixon had made a significant toast during his unprecedented 1972 visit to China.

This pattern, which continued throughout my visit, led me to recognize the depth and lasting impact that Nixon and Secretary of State Henry Kissinger made during their journey there. Just like today, if a Democratic president had made that visit then, the right-wingers would have eviscerated whomever had reached out to "Communist China."

My Chinese hosts, who also became my friends, felt an incredible sense of pride and self-worth because the leader of the free world had honored them with his presence. If the North Korean media provide the story factually to their audiences, then perhaps the citizens of that country might also experience a similar sense of dignity and respect as result.

My wish for hope may be naive based on the unpredictable, impolitic and often discourteous behavior of our president. But, even if the chances are slim, I'm pulling for him ... and, for all of us ... this time.

CULTURE-CHANGING ACTIONS BY HASLAM THAT ARE UNDER THE RADAR

APRIL 2, 2019

CULTURE-CHANGING ACTIONS BY HASLAM
THAT ARE UNDER THE RADAR
By Bo Roberts

As the sand runs out on the Bill Haslam gubernatorial time clock, there were two major accomplishments during his eight years that few recognize, but which will change the culture of state government and higher education.

Gov. Haslam's major achievements, particularly in education, have rightly been praised in these pages and nationally, as well. A prime example is the bold and innovative Tennessee Promise program. Originally created as an initiative offering free tuition to Tennessee community colleges and colleges of applied technologies, the Promise program was later supplemented with ReConnect, permitting adults to start or return to those institutions without paying. Further, our state has also been lauded for its rate of academic achievement in grades K-12.

The changes I am referring to were accomplished, quietly and without much fanfare, early on in Haslam's administration.

First is the TEAM Act that updated and altered the state's longstanding Civil Service laws to allow state managers to

146

actually reward those who demonstrated quality performanc-
es while sending messages to those who weren't. It sounds so
simple, but many in management fought or resented it because,
heaven forbid, it made them manage. For example, it was much
easier to make across-the-board increases in salaries than to
make judgment calls about skill sets.

Only time will tell how effective and impactful that culture-changing act will be applied and what the results are, but,
the fact is, that Gov. Haslam and his administration addressed
the issue and instituted a more effective management system
throughout state government with its 43,500 employees.

The second major shift in the way state business is conducted has affected all levels of public higher education. The
First to the Top Act (passed through the bipartisan efforts of
former Governor Phil Bredesen and a GOP-controlled General
Assembly) was not only fully embraced by the incoming Haslam
administration, but served as a launch pad for a series of other
comprehensive education initiatives....demonstrating a rare
case of policy triumphing over partisanship or ideology.

First to the Top altered the allocation of funds formula for
higher education so that it was based (GASP!) on production or
successes of those students. How many of those students who
started, actually got a degree or a certificate at that campus?
Surprise... institutions which suddenly began doing a better job
would be rewarded more than those which did not ....another

culture-altering change which led many to applaud and some to shudder.

Added to those changes, Haslam and the General Assembly appropriated (for the first time in years) more actual dollars to implement this new formula. Plus, with the encouragement from higher education advisor Randy Boyd (now coincidentally serving as interim president of the University of Tennessee), the Drive to 55 initiative seeking to increase the number of college graduates in Tennessee hit the road at full speed.

Hopefully, in my eyes at least, these improvements will be reinforced, studied, measured and possibly even improved upon in future administrations and general assemblies.

Kudos and thanks to Gov. Haslam and his administration for not only addressing these issues, but for taking definitive action to improve our state. No governor is perfect, and none will be, but Bill Haslam is a good and decent man who faced challenges head-on in his own genteel manner and made a difference for many generations to come. Thanks, Bill.

GOVERNOR BILL HASLAM,

served as Tennessee's chief executive from 2011-2019.

(Photo courtesy of Gov. Haslam's office)

TAKING CARE OF BUSINESS
Deputy Governor Jim Henry leaving a meeting
with Governor Bill Haslam, right, and Henry's successor as
Commissioner of Children's Services Bonnie Hommrich.
(Photo courtesy of Jim Henry)

VIII. THE ROARING TWENTIES
COLUMNS 2020-2022

JULY WEEKEND MARKED END OF A SIGNIFICANT ERA
AUGUST 5, 2020

JULY WEEKEND MARKED END OF A SIGNIFICANT ERA

By Bo Roberts

Tennessee headed for embarrassing Senate representation

A long, impressive era of noteworthy U.S. senate representation in the Volunteer State is hurtling headlong towards its demise, as was illustrated so pointedly over the July Fourth weekend.

It is the end of literate, ethical, non-partisan strain of politics that began with and encompassed the essence of the brilliantly diplomatic Sen. Howard Baker. Three recent occurrences slapped me (figuratively) right in the face:

–The state's senior senator, Lamar Alexander, had a thoughtful, reasoned op-ed about why former President Andrew Jackson of Tennessee should be honored despite a litany of faults. Sen. Alexander had his start in politics and government on the staff of Sen. Baker. His announced retirement means he will be the last of the Baker legacy come January.

– Junior senator Marsha Blackburn also had an op-ed published on Sunday, which was a xenophobic attack crafted to instill fear. I couldn't help but wonder if it was actually written by someone on President

Trump's staff. The column was a perfect reflection of a career dedicated to divisive dogma.

– Senate GOP-candidate/wannabe Bill Hagerty had a television commercial that I saw several times over the weekend jumping on the divisive team. He had the gall to oxymoronically use "rule of law" as a belief while touting Trump's endorsement. I didn't happen to see any of Dr, Manny Sethi's commercials over the weekend, but previous ones, though a little slicker, were mainly promoting his stringent divisive credentials, as well. Even though military veteran James Mackler is an attractive and well-qualified candidate and will be the Democratic nominee, one of the two Republicans will likely bookend the Howard Baker era.

I had the good fortune to get to know Howard Baker early in my career while editing the newspapers in Sevier County. My next door neighbor, Johnny Waters, was Baker's campaign manager the first time he ran, and lost, and the second time when he was elected to the senate. Though members of different parties, there were no barriers to communication and I learned he had two main considerations in exercising his duties: What's best for the country, and what's best for Tennessee? The two rarely conflicted.

Later in my career as Chief of Staff to a Democratic governor and CEO of the 1982 World's Fair in Knoxville, I had multiple opportunities to work with this charismatic, effective and powerful lawyer from tiny Huntsville, TN, who, in just my interactions with him, was so helpful and produced such positive energy and results. I know I'm prejudiced, but if there were a Mount Rushmore of Tennessee's outstanding contributors, Howard Baker would be on it.

His "strain" produced reasoned and reasonable leaders like Winfield Dunn, Lamar Alexander, Bob Corker, Fred Thompson, Don Sundquist, Bill Frist, and Bill Haslam. All of them worked across the partisan aisle to shape our exceptional state. While I, and others didn't agree with everything, anyone who knew them knew they were going to try to do the right thing for Tennessee.

I also know the many Democratic senators and governors who worked with Sen. Baker over the years held him in particularly high esteem. And, though I disagree with many of their policies, I am optimistic that our current state leaders have the core values that reflect some of the Baker approach

For the sake of the children and grandchildren of all of us, I truly hope the next Howard Baker is now emerging somewhere. We have never needed them more.

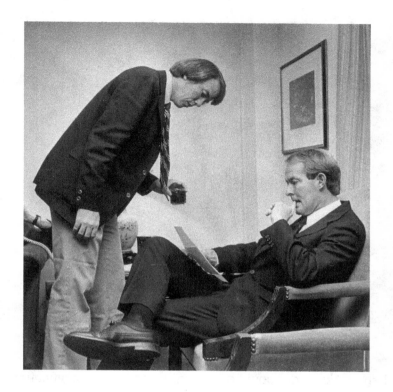

EARLY RETURNS

Top aide Tom Ingram, left, gives candidate Lamar Alexander
an early voting report for the 1978 gubernatorial election.
Alexander would win his first election and serve two terms
(1979-1987) as governor, before being elected U.S. Senator from
Tennessee, where he served three terms (2003-2021).
Ingram, who was named the first Deputy to the Governor,
would later form the Ingram Group,
a formidable political force in the state.
(Photo courtesy of Tom Ingram)

SERVICE AGAIN AND AGAIN

Lamar Alexander could be described as the personification
of service to his home state Tennessee and the nation.
In the early days, the East Tennessee Republican served as a staff
member to Senator Howard Baker, prior to his election
(on his second try) as governor of Tennessee in 1978.
Following two productive gubernatorial terms (1979-1997),
and a stint as U.S. Secretary of Education,
Alexander was elected to the U.S. Senate three times (2003-2021).
A move Alexander made during his second term was unprecedented—
he resigned as chairman of the important Senate Republican
Conference, so that he could devote his attention to the bi-partisan
educational issues that were his passion.

PANDEMIC PERSPECTIVE

DECEMBER 7, 2020

PANDEMIC PERSPECTIVE
By Bo Roberts

> *Dec. 7, 1941 (Invasion of Pearl Harbor): Deaths–2,035*
>
> *Sep. 11, 2001 (Invasion of New York): Deaths–2,996*
>
> *Dec. 3, 2020 (One day in COVID invasion of U.S.): Deaths-2,857*
>
> *World War II: Total U.S. deaths: 407,316 in 3½ years*
>
> *COVID-19: Total U.S. deaths as Dec. 6, 2020: 281,000 in 9 months*
>
> *Projected total of COVID-19 deaths after one year: 400,000 +*
>
> *(Total number of deaths in U.S. as of August, 2023: 1,100,000)*

As we observe the "Day that shall live in infamy" some of us actually remember the day the U.S. Naval base in Honolulu was victim of a sneak attack by the Japanese air force. Most of us well remember the impact of 9-11 and how it changed the way we, as Americans, view safety and travel.

Since March, all of us have been living through the invasion of an invisible, yet lethal virus. Statistics tell us a lot, but do they impact us personally? Other than totally changing a lot of the way I lived my life, and how respectful I am of taking every caution possible, it became even more personal last week when my wife's father succumbed to COVID-19.

I have had close friends who have suffered and survived this wicked invader, but this was the first actual death to directly hit our family. You may have heard about the Gold Star banners that hung in the windows of those families who lost loved ones during World War II. I wonder what our streets would look like now if every family hung a banner with a colored star to signify their loss?

An additional perspective: The number of COVID-19 deaths we have already had in our country exceeds the total number of all deaths in the U.S. Navy, Marines and Coast Guard in World War II.

Like you, I'm sure, I celebrate the wave of hope we are getting about the vaccine and, if we cooperate, we could be able to return to some kind of new normal next year.

Until then, we can reduce the number of death "statistics" by doing things I don't believe those who gave their lives to one of our wars would call tough: wear a mask, socially distance, and wash your hands.

Statistics don't lie, especially when they become so very personal.

OUR FRAGILE DEMOCRACY CALLS FOR FORMIDABLE REPUBLICANS

FEBRUARY 8, 2021

**OUR FRAGILE DEMOCRACY CALLS
FOR FORMIDABLE REPUBLICANS
By Bo Roberts**

A modest, honorable, former Republican president leaned in close to a modest, honorable, congressional Democrat leader, and, speaking through his face mask, said: "Joe Biden is the only one who could have been elected."

Those words, relayed by receiver Rep. Jim Clyburn of S.C., stood out most amidst all the immensely moving speeches, poems and songs heard on Inauguration Day 2021. Rep. Clyburn is generally acknowledged as "the one" who delivered the essential Palmetto State to Biden during the Democratic primary. It was that momentum that enabled Biden to dramatically cinch the Democratic nomination for president.

The powerful words Clyburn heard came from former Republican president George W. Bush, who had long made it clear that he was never a fan of then-President Trump. I strongly believe that Bush was absolutely correct, and, though I was 100% for former VP Biden from Day One, I still felt the alarm that Bush's words engendered.

To think that a moderate (and, more importantly a decent human being who had a track record of honesty and integrity) was the only one who could beat such a despicable human being—who clearly brought out the worst in people—-was truly frightening. Even in losing, Trump brought out the worst in so many people...particularly members and leaders of his own party.

Nearly every Republican office holder was cowed by Trump's "base;" a base that was expanded by bringing in those who were not part of any party: every violent group that wasn't like them....white, angry, straight, against anyone who wasn't like them, anti-Semitic, vulgar, and, I would add, slightly stupid and gullible. Those groups were the ones Trump first allowed in, while encouraging and inflaming their rage and prejudice, before finally inciting them to a deadly insurrection at our national capitol building. They are part of the "base" that brought literal fear to the figurative fear Trump had been using against his own party for years.

Think about it: had that group of rioting hoodlums been just a bit smarter and a tad more organized, what was a deadly catastrophe on January 6th could have been a disaster on par with or exceeding any sneak attack by a foreign country.

Frankly, I do not believe the crisis is behind us. As a lifelong Democrat (who strongly believes our nation needs a strong Republican Party with which I can vigorously work against), I can accept losing to a candidate with whom I disagree but yet respect. We are a long way from that with the shadow of Trump still looming large. We need to do what then-Majority Senate Leader Mitch McConnell indicated regarding the party ridding itself of Trump (and I assume his violent, hateful friends) and admitting that he incited the rioting at our nation's capital.

At first I thought the exercise of impeachment was a waste of time, and would unnecessarily keep the focus on Trump when we need to be addressing the urgent needs our nation faces. Now, though unlikely, there is a chance to do what Leader McConnell asked.

If only 12 Republican senators join the five who supported a procedural vote on impeachment, they could convict a tyrant. And, though already out of office, the most important next step would be to ban Trump from ever running for office again.

The current Republicans need to call on the spirit of celebrated diplomat and extraordinary lawmaker Howard Baker (a hero to this Democrat and multitudes of others), and the strength of such outstanding former

Tennessee GOP leaders like Bob Corker, Bill Haslam, Bill Frist, John Duncan, Bill Jenkins, and Beth Harwell to lend them the courage and conviction necessary to do what's right.

If Senator McConnell can convince just 11 others (out of 45) to stand up for their Party and this country, then we could all celebrate the grandest victory for the survival of America and democracy since the Battle of Appomattox Court House in 1865.

The chance begins on February 9. God help us all.

AN OPEN LETTER TO FIRST LADY (AND FIRST TEACHER) JILL BIDEN

JUNE 30, 2021

AN OPEN LETTER TO FIRST LADY
(AND FIRST TEACHER) JILL BIDEN
By Bo Roberts

Our country must make a direct investment in the very people who have the future of our society in their hands—K-12 public school teachers.

Dear madam first lady:

I am writing to you, really, as the nation's first teacher.

I have a proposal/recommendation that I sincerely believe would have a dramatic influence on your esteemed profession, not to mention your devotion and passion for the field.

As influenced by my 12th-grade English teacher, Clarice Bunch, a mentor and an inspiration, I am going to do my best here to keep it simple. My idea is born of Congress' bipartisan act, agreed to and signed by a Republican president, to provide $2.6 trillion in response to the COVID-19 pandemic and its disastrous economic impact.

Specifically, my idea is about the portion of that bill that appropriated a $600 per week add-on for those who were eligible to receive unemployment insurance payments. I fully supported that program. In 11 weeks, some 25.6 million Americans

162

received more than $230 billion in payments. I thought, Wow! This country truly understands how to address an unprecedented crisis in an extraordinary way.

As the pandemic grew into a tragedy of a magnitude beyond what could have possibly been envisioned, America took decisive action again and again. I kept wondering what we could do to acknowledge a need we have collectively attempted in every way possible to avoid throughout our history. The answer? Make a direct investment in the very people who have the future of our society in their hands — K-12 public school teachers.

Experts, consultants, and congressional and administration staff regularly devise plans and programs, tests and measurements, etc., though I dare say that none of them would consider working for what an average teacher earns in the U.S. Do we value the teaching profession that is at the core, the heart and soul of what happens to our children and grandchildren? Clearly not enough.

$600 per month per teacher

So here's my proposal for consideration: Let's invest $600 a month (not a week) in our teachers across the board, no strings attached, direct to their bank accounts. The average salary for a U.S. teacher is $61,730. A $7,200 payment would amount to an 11.6% increase. Because the average starting salary is just

$38,617, the add-on would be 18.6% — potentially enough to change an 18-year-old's mind about becoming a teacher when entering college, or maybe keep an experienced teacher in the profession.

(Reminder to me from Mrs. Bunch: Keep it simple.)

Let teachers know we value them

And possibly just as important, our country would be sending a direct message to teachers: You are valued.

Hear more Tennessee voices: Get the weekly opinion newsletter for insightful and thought-provoking columns.

The cost to do that is about $23 billion. Yes, that's a mighty big sum. Less than 1% of just the money in the first bill referenced above, or a little more than it would cost to build two aircraft carriers (yes, we all love aircraft carriers). Stated another way, the money it took to fund those 11 weeks of payments would pay for 10 years of the $7,200 annual raises for teachers.

Now, madam first teacher, I know you and your family have a lot on your plate; that might be the understatement of the year! However, I can't stop believing that something so simple would serve as a deep inspiration for the current and future generations of your fellow teachers.

Some disclaimers: I am not nor have I ever been a teacher. I am a small-business owner who has no direct or indirect ties to the profession. I do have a son and daughter-in-law who have just retired as public school teachers.

Before finalizing my thoughts on this, I talked to a few honored teachers I knew would be straight with me. They unanimously supported the idea while saying that I was a little crazy to invest time pursuing it. But here we are. I trust that you will have the opportunity to read this and make your own judgment. I did write this in advance of your husband's first speech before Congress and his reveal of the details of the American

Families Plan, which is a wonderful, bold investment in our future. I am not asking this as an add-on, but as negotiations move forward it could possibly be squeezed into the educational considerations.

The power of a good teacher

I keep thinking about Mrs. Bunch, a diminutive, exquisitely dressed lady who could strike fear and silence in a room of students by just tapping her foot. She also taught my dad. He told me how he had experienced that same fear many decades earlier. Our mutual respect for Mrs. Bunch endured far beyond the years in which she was our teacher. I know she would be exceptionally pleased that a teacher became America's first lady.

God bless you and your family. And say thanks from me to a member of your family who always says "God bless our troops." As a veteran, I feel valued.

Thanks to recent Belmont University graduate Emily Vo for her research on this project.

TOP QUESTION FOR LEGISLATURE: WBFT?

OCTOBER 22, 2021

TOP QUESTION FOR LEGISLATURE: WBFT?
By Bo Roberts

There are only a few times in an office holder's career that a milestone moment arrives when the primary question should be: What's Best for Tennessee? (WBFT?)

One of those times is this week during the General Assembly's special session called by Gov. Bill Lee. It offers a chance to make a bold, bipartisan statement demonstrating that employment opportunities benefit every Tennessean, no matter where the jobs may be located.

The leaders of both houses are expected to do more than simply lead their respective party; their responsibility is to *every* resident of the Volunteer State. They will have two forthcoming occasions to show their allegiance to that higher principle.

But first, the one this week: as someone who grew up in East Tennessee, and has resided in Nashville for the last 30 years, I am ecstatic that our fellow Tennesseans in the western part of the state are finally reaping the rewards of years of dedicated efforts by many. It took both governors and legislators, from each party, to envision and develop the Memphis Regional Megasite where Ford Motor Company and its South Korean partners' multi-billion-dollar project will create more than 5,800 well-paying jobs.

We should all commend the outstanding work done by ECD Commissioner Bob Rolfe and his professional colleagues, who ultimately closed a deal that had been years-in-the-making. During the first half of the 1980s, then-Gov. Lamar Alexander (1979-1987), a Republican, worked hand-in-glove with a Democratic-controlled legislature to shift the automobile industry's focus toward investing in our state, as did then-Gov. Phil Bredesen (2003-2011), a Democrat, working side-by-side with former Sen. Bob Corker, Republican from Chattanooga, and others, to entice Volkswagen's enormous investment in that part of the state.

In every instance, the fundamental question that they asked themselves was this: WBFT?

This week's special session will allow us to ratify, once again, the success of our politicians' past collaborations by recognizing and cementing the current potential prosperity shining before us.

The next opportunity for monumental action will come sometime after the first of the year, when committees will bring forth plans charting the political landscape of the next generation, called redistricting. Decisions made now will reverberate in the lives of all Tennesseans for the next decade, at least.

The rumors now circulating about the highly partisan game-playing in designing our nine congressional districts are quite disturbing. Yes, there's a partisan opening to slap Davidson County in the face and shred the state's main economic engine of the past 10 years. Invoking such a perniciously partisan political measure, however, will irreparably damage the very companies which have devoted extraordinary amounts of their resources to our state.

To think that Davidson County, our state's capital city and a cradle of economic and creative energy, would not have its own congressional district would be more than a travesty; it would be an embarrassment of extreme significance.

This column is not about 5th District Congressman Jim Cooper. Though I consider Cooper a friend and a brilliant civil servant, this issue is far more wide-reaching than one person serving a two-year term in Washington; it would be a devastating move which would quickly erode the economic euphoria from which we Tennesseans have all so greatly benefited.

I understand just how tempting it could be to convene a room full of like-minded thinkers to engage in Ouidja board redistricting games with numbers and geography. But, beware, those numbers could easily erase Tennessee's vast good fortune, which has been the envy of legions of lawmakers across the nation.

When leaders are guided by a WBFT philosophy, the resulting decisions are uncomplicated, simple, and appropriate for all.

I implore our leaders to ask: WBFT?

(*The Tennessee legislature redistricted Davidson County to include three congressional districts and is now represented in Congress by three Republicans, none of whom live in Nashville/ Davidson County.*)

BIPARTISAN TURMOIL, NUCLEAR OPTION SAVED VOLUNTEER STATE'S REPUTATION

JANUARY 8, 2022

BIPARTISAN TURMOIL, NUCLEAR OPTION SAVED VOLUNTEER STATE'S REPUTATION

By Bo Roberts

Nearly 50 years ago this week, in an unexpected move, five veteran Democratic state senators bolted away from their caucus, joining their minority GOP colleagues to re-elect Bill Snodgrass as the Comptroller of the state of Tennessee. In the view of many, their uncommon action was a textbook example of cooler heads prevailing, as their votes were crucial in preserving the financial integrity of Tennessee.

A few might argue with my assessment, but most would agree that partisan turmoil virtually exploded when the 85th General Assembly convened in Nashville on January 3, 1973. With five senate defections, the brilliant, unflappable Snodgrass was returned to his position by a vote of 66 to 63, besting Democratic Caucus-nominee Floyd Kephart.

To understand the significance of that vote, it helps to know the background of how such a dramatic situation evolved. To describe the national state of affairs in America in 1968 as being "in turmoil" would be far too tame. Legendary rights leader Martin Luther King had been assassinated in our state in

April, while Sen. Bobby Kennedy had been assassinated in June in Los Angeles. The Democratic National Convention in Chicago in August was riled by thousands of Vietnam War protestors and marked by bloodshed with the National Guard called in to help quell the unrest. And, in November, Democratic presidential nominee Hubert Humphrey finished behind soon-to-be President-elect

Republican Richard Nixon and Independent George Wallace in Tennessee, as the state GOP gained a slight (49-49-1) edge in our House of Representatives.

The political shift in the Volunteer State was seismic as it led to the election of the first Republican Speaker of the House, Bill Jenkins, since Reconstruction (1865-1877). As the Chief of Staff to then-Governor Buford Ellington (D), I can attest that nothing really changed. We worked with Speaker Jenkins (who went on to serve as Congressman from the

First Congressional District before being appointed as a Federal Judge). Looking back, I would characterize the cooperation between the two factions as amazing and rewarding, and, perhaps, even a bit surprising when compared to the political landscape of today.

The next statewide election saw another major shift when Memphis dentist and Republican-nominee Winfield Dunn upset John J. Hooker in 1970 to become Tennessee's first GOP governor in 50 years. The state returned a Democrat majority to the House of Representatives with a firebrand, extremely partisan Jim McKinney from Nashville elected as Speaker of the House. At the same time, John Wilder, a soft-spoken Senator from Somerville, began his decades-long reign as Speaker of the Senate and Lt. Governor.

Having suddenly pivoted away from a strong governor-controlled government, the first two years of Gov. Dunn's administration saw an independent legislature running amok. Of monumental importance, laws were changed to hand the speakers of the two houses shared appointive powers for nearly every board or commission in the state.

Speaker McKinney's heavy-handed, highly partisan rule was challenged after the 1972 elections. Following a brutal battle, the wily, gentle giant Ned McWherter prevailed by one vote in the Democratic caucus to become the Speaker nominee. He quickly reestablished civility and practiced a mantra of "What's Best for Tennessee" during the remainder of Gov. Dunn's term, and throughout two terms of progress under Gov. Lamar Alexander (1979-1987), before serving as governor himself for two terms (1987-1995).

However, during that tumultuous one-vote caucus win, some younger members of the House and Senate caucuses were convinced that the Office of Comptroller was not partisan *enough*, and voted to back the young and bright, but highly partisan Floyd (Skeeter) Kephart as their nominee.

Here's where the "nuclear option" referenced in the headline appears. I had returned to the University of Tennessee in 1971, with no plans to deal directly with the state legislature. However, some internal issues had arisen at UT's Medical Units in Memphis. Then-UT President Ed Boling dispatched my fellow vice president, Dr. Joe Johnson to deal with the situation as interim Chancellor, so I picked up Johnson's duties as UT's lobbyist in Nashville.

Due to Speaker McKinney's strong anti-UT position, it was quite a raucous experience; I was not sad about the change in the House leadership. Though I was not involved, I was disturbed to see Kephart's nomination. I had a close friendship with Bill Snodgrass, who, along with Harlan Mathews, state Commissioner of Finance and Administration, had been patient mentors to this young guy serving under Gov. Ellington. Snodgrass and Mathews were, undoubtedly, the architects of

Tennessee's exceptional reputation as the best fiscally managed state in the U.S. The "nuclear option" employed on that Wednesday in 1973 became the bedrock of the hard-earned reputation which Tennessee still enjoys to this day.

The credit for their courage and foresight was ascribed to the late, veteran senators Milton Hamilton of Union City, Bill Baird of Lebanon, Ray Baird of Rockwood, J. Reagor Motlow of Lynchburg, and Halbert Harvill of Clarksville, and to my former colleague, the astute Dick Barry of Lexington (former Speaker of the House with whom I served in Gov. Ellington's cabinet), who deftly managed the delicate orchestration of the "nuclear option" operation.

After all the wildness of that session, and despite several threats to "get back at Snodgrass," in 1975, the General Assembly unanimously re-elected Bill Snodgrass as the state's Comptroller. He went on to serve in that capacity for more than 43 years, spanning the administrations of seven governors and 23 General Assemblies.

One of those General Assemblies celebrated his storied legacy by naming the state's largest building, yes, you guessed it...drumroll, please: the William R. Snodgrass Tower.

Should the 112th General Assembly need a dose of measured guidance when it convenes on Capitol Hill tomorrow, a quick glance toward the monumental Snodgrass building on 7th Avenue will serve as a reminder that bipartisanship, combined with fiscal responsibility, are always good ideas.

CELEBRATING BIPARTISANSHIP AT ITS TENNESSEE BEST

SEPTEMBER 1, 2022

CELEBRATING BIPARTISANSHIP AT ITS TENNESSEE BEST
By Bo Roberts

The 1982 World's Fair in Knoxville was the most successful authorized international exposition in the U.S. since the 1933 Chicago World's Fair.

Facts: The event had more countries participating (23) and the highest attendance (11.4 million visitors) than the space themed Seattle World's Fair in 1962, San Antonio's Hemisfair in 1968, the environmental themed event in Spokane, WA in 1974, and the succeeding international event in New Orleans in 1984. There haven't been any in the U.S. since then.

Opinion: The 184-day extravaganza in East Tennessee would not have happened without the unbelievable depth of support from Republican and Democratic officials at the local, state, and federal levels, which impacted the international community as well.

Full Disclosure: My views may be a bit biased in that I was the president and CEO of the non-profit corporation that organized and conducted the event. I am proud to have been associated with a group of office holders, business and labor leaders, who stood together to collectively answer the question all got at some time: "You're doing a what? Where?" Let's examine some more facts:

Local: The office of mayor in Knoxville is a nonpartisan office, but the mayor in 1975 when the idea was presented was an aggressive Republican (Kyle Testerman) who adopted the challenge, and wisely appointed two banking and political leaders (Jake Butcher, owner of East Tennessee's largest bank and a major Democrat player and fundraiser, and Jim Haslam, associated with the second largest bank in East Tennessee and a well-known Republican fundraiser and king maker) to head up the study committee. While the matter was being studied, an upstart young Democrat (Randy Tyree) ran for mayor and by 37 votes got into a runoff and then beat the incumbent. He picked up the mantle of leadership for the World's Fair, and along with five of the nine City Council members (not sure of their party affiliation but I think three Republicans and two Democrats) passed the authorization of $11.6 million to purchase the site). Without both of these leaders, the event would not have happened.

State: A Democrat (Ray Blanton) was governor and though there was no love lost between he and I nor he and Butcher, his administration provided enough help for us to stay alive. Then the race for governor to succeed the scandal-ridden Blanton, boiled down to (gasp) a bright young Republican named Lamar Alexander from Maryville and the chairman of our board, Butcher, who resigned for the race, Haslam took over as chairman and when Butcher lost, without hardly a ripple, Haslam stepped back to vice chairman and Butcher was reinstated as chairman. AND, with all that Gov. Alexander provided great leadership, worked with the Democratically controlled legislature and the totally necessary state involvement was great.

National: The application for the event started under Republican president Gerald Ford, then continued and had the support from Democrat Pres. Jimmy Carter, who invited the world when we were improved internationally, and then Republican Pres. Ronald Reagan, with the urging and support of Majority Leader Howard Baker and Knoxville congressman John Duncan, threw his support behind the effort and was there to speak at the opening ceremony on May 1, 1982.

And this brief summary, is just the tip of an iceberg of intrigue, challenges, a mere sampling of the kind of support that it took to provide this, in my view, joyous occasion for millions of people. It wasn't just

Knoxville that flourished during a national recession, Opryland Theme Park, for example, had its largest attendance ever, venues all across the state set records that year, the KY horse themed state park on I-75 north of Knoxville had a record year with 500% increase in attendance, and Asheville, NC housed and sent 90 busloads a day to the event that averaged about 63,000 attendance each day (peaking at 102,000 on Oct. 9).

One cannot question the impact, the long-term value is being celebrated, discussed and debated in Knoxville through this year. But I don't think anyone could dispute that it happened because leaders from both parties led and were joined by leaders from the private sector to meet a common goal.

40th anniversary of 1982 World's Fair, the largest tourism event in TN history could not have happened without both parties working together at all levels

PRESIDENTIAL OPENING

President Ronald Reagan officially opens the 1982 World's Fair
in Knoxville with First Lady Nancy Reagan and the author,
along with dignitaries from around the world.

SASSER BRIEFING

Author briefs Democratic Senator Jim Sasser
about the 1982 World's Fair. A moderate, Sasser served
from 1977-1995, prior to his appointment as Ambassador
to China by President Bill Clinton.

BAKER UPDATE

Author reviews the scale-model of the World's Fair site with Senator
Howard Baker, before a reception hosted by Secretary of State
Alexander M. Haig, Jr. in Washington, D. C.

LEIGH HENDRY

Editor

(Photo courtesy of Jerry Atnip)

NASHVILLE'S SUCCESS WITH PUBLIC PROJECTS SHOWS WHY NEW TITANS STADIUM WILL WORK
DECEMBER 15, 2022

In the last 25 years, two seismic waves of historic change swept through our city, collectively giving us the Nashville of today — the 2.0.22 version. Another wave is now quickly rolling forward, ready to break onto our shores. Think of it as a wall of monumental opportunity.

It's a chance to fully revamp and refine the entire East Bank of our city; to completely re-imagine a part of downtown Nashville that has rarely been the focus of much creative energy or planning expertise.

With the advent of a climate-controlled, state-of-the-art sports facility as its anchor, the East Bank's "Cinderella" moment could finally be arriving.

How the Tennessee Titans ownership fits in

With the possibility of a new stadium, the obvious elephants in the development room are the Tennessee Titans and owner representative Amy Adams Strunk. She has fully embraced her ownership role, loosened the team's purse strings and become a highly visible part of the Nashville and Tennessee communities.

The team's leadership has partnered with Mayor John Cooper in proposing innovative solutions to a looming issue, while recommending exciting possibilities for both the facility and the region.

Frankly, this enlightened approach would not have happened in the older traditional ways most NFL owners conducted business. I, and many others, are greatly impressed with the plan outlined by Titans' President Burke Nihill, the prime presenter of a plan that will swing doors wide for a multitude of appealing prospects. Thank you, Amy, for opening those doors.

Music City Center was the last "largest" public project

At more than $2.1 billion, the new stadium under consideration would represent the largest public endeavor ever undertaken in Tennessee. Meanwhile, there's much to learn by reviewing the last significant project here that carried that "historic" label: Music City Center.

Following Metro Council's approval in 2010, this standout venue opened for business in 2013.

There were countless doubters 12 years ago when the Metro Council debated a $600 million price tag for a convention center located in a less-than-pristine area of downtown. Following his 2007 election as mayor, Karl Dean and his staff dove head-first into the myriad plans and projections, before going all in to spearhead "this major investment" in Nashville's future.

Bridgestone Arena started the ball rolling

Dean's gigantic step came more than a decade after then-Mayor Phil Bredesen initiated plans for a downtown entertainment and sports arena, fostering a new Hilton Hotel, the Country Music Hall of Fame, and, ultimately, the Schermerhorn Symphony Center.

Bredesen's investment paid enormous dividends, particularly after the Nashville Predator's local ownership recruited a first-rank management team led by Sean Henry.

The partnership between the Nashville Sports Authority (the arena's public landlord) and Henry transformed the arena into one of the finest, top-performing entertainment venues in the world.

Music City Center blew the doors off

How could the Music Center follow that incredible feat? In step with the tourism industry, MCC president and CEO Charles Stark and his staff quickly had the center operating at capacity, one of the few such facilities turning an operating profit in the U.S. Additionally, throughout the pandemic, when business had vanished, they retained their employees at full pay, *and* carved out more than $113 million for Metro Government to assist in addressing citizens' needs during those most challenging times.

The success stories about the space-strained MCC go on and on, but let me sum it up in one additional (to me startling) sentence: When the MCC opened its doors for conventions in

2013, the number of hotel rooms available within their convention footprint was 3,900; that total reached more than 15,000 last month after more than 2200 conventions, 4.2 million unique attendees and a phenomenal $3 billion in economic impact!

This is why I, and scores of others, are encouraging Metro Council members to do their due diligence, while keeping their eyes on the actual overall costs amid the positive opportunities that will emerge. Council should consider the unprecedented $500 million appropriation from the state (thanks to Gov. Bill Lee, Lt. Gov. Randy McNally, House Speaker Cameron Sexton and the General Assembly). All of that and with this major step forward the funding burden will be placed on stadium users and visitors, rather than Davidson County's taxpayers.

And forward, this time, means attracting top-tier events like the Super Bowl, the Final Four, college playoff games, major championships and all-weather concerts and events, while simultaneously providing citizens with a vastly superior quality of life on our East Bank. Nashville's recent history with these kinds of undertakings should give us extraordinary confidence in our ability to forge our future.

IX. MOVING FORWARD AND FIGHTING THE FIGHT

I hope your journey along this thought process trail hasn't diverted readers from my original mission: To keep a "flaming" passion regarding efforts to reach "moderate," or reasoned conclusions, that yield effective results.

As I was writing this in the fall of 2023, a cluster of "clowns to the left" and a jam-up of "jokers to the right" abounded, a cavalcade of grandstanders, with few of them deserving "RESPECT." They definitely haven't achieved much in turns of "RESULTS." Every election seems to represent another turning point in our nation's history. Will 2024 be like that, too, but on steroids? I think the "clowns" have been somewhat muffled by the moderation of a persuasive nominee, incumbent President Joe Biden. Chronologically challenged though he may be, Biden remains an energetic octogenarian.

The battle for the middle ground is against the "jokers" who demand that their candidate lean farther and farther right in order to emerge triumphant in the Republican primary. Though there are not many more loyal Democrats, I fervently and wistfully hope that a. John McCain or a Mitt Romney or a Jeb Bush-type, who is reasoned and reasonable might yet emerge. Certainly that candidate will need an extremely thick coat of armor to repel the clowns' vicious attacks. They will also need to articulate a crystal-clear message in order to penetrate the "wall of right wing shame."

If (and, oh, what a big *if* it is) our nation is lucky enough to elect a reasonable individual it will represent a major step in the desired direction. But, the battle will not be over, not by a long shot.

Generations of what I call the "Koch Brothers States' Stampede" cannot be easily undone. I say that in the sense of what has historically been the most defining, successful, and polarizing political movement in my lifetime. We now have an unfathomable number of local and state officials laser-focused on partisan and ideological issues (abortion, anti-LGBQT issues, guns, race, libraries, etc.) instead of things that truly matter in our society: education, jobs, transit, environment, safety and health.

Hopefully, positive results at the top will embolden more and more candidates, young and old, to enter the arena of public service for all the right reasons.

* * *

"Power tends to corrupt and absolute power corrupts absolutely," British politician and essayist Lord Acton wrote in an 1887 letter. His thoughts reflected the concurring opinions of the legion of essayists observing the monarchical ebbs and flow of his day.

Through Acton's now-famous quote didn't make its public debut until 1907, more than 100 years later, it remains exceedingly relevant.

And, it certainly reflects the tenor of the times in Tennessee and other Koch-won states. As the majority's ethical violations were mostly being swept under the Capitol Hill rug, the march of absolute power took a slight punch in the nose during the 2023 legislative session. With unchecked power to do most anything, the Tennessee House of Representatives expelled two of its Black members. The men were accused of disrupting a legislative session by encouraging a protesting audience. The protest group, composed primarily of mothers, was enraged about a recent school shooting in Nashville that had left six dead, including three nine-year-olds. The tragedy became a national issue, mushrooming overnight into an international news story. Both Black legislators were eventually returned to office by their local officials who still had the power to determine who would fill vacancies.

Amidst the uproar, divisive opinions and accusations within the ruling Tennessee GOP delegation were exposed. Was this just a temporary blip or a possible slight turning point? Might this lead to a more (God forbid the thought) MODERATE group of office holders who would spend their time addressing needs and opportunities rather than attacking and inflaming constituents? Sadly, probably not. Some reasonable moderates do remain in office; but imagining this altercation resulting in a sweeping change would be illusionary, I'm afraid.

To have even a slight FLAME of hope, however, is encouraging.

I can visualize the scintilla of hope that swelled in the hearts of many in the 1950s, as the accusatory espionage hearings of the reckless Wisconsin Senator Joe McCarthy were winding down. After wrecking the lives of thousands, the hearings disintegrated before finally concluding this sordid episode in America's history. Ironically, while writing this, my wife and I had just visited the historic American Library in Paris. I was making a presentation at the institution, which was founded in 1920 with thousands of books shipped from the U.S. for American troops during World War I. The library survived World War II, including the Nazi invasion and the capture of France. Throughout Germany's occupation, the library staff secretly distributed books to Jews, risking arrest and imprisonment. Years later, the library's heroic, resilient culture was still in evidence as its leaders refused to allow infamous McCarthy henchman Roy Cohn and his cohorts to enter the building. They had invaded

Paris to see what kind of "Commie" books Americans were disseminating. That library has survived and still thrives. It's a beacon of hope for other libraries, blacks, immigrants, women, gays, Muslims, theme parks like Disney and other oppressed people and "differents." We as a nation have also survived and will continue to do so because the good people find ways to prevail.

There was another ember of hope that flamed briefly following our return from Paris. A bi-partisan (*bi-partisan!*) vote in both houses of Congress resulted in the avoidance of a disastrous economic calamity when it passed a compromise (repeat *compromise!*) bill to raise the U.S. debt ceiling. Republican House Speaker Kevin McCarthy managed to cobble together an agreement with President Joe Biden, a solution achieved only by each ceding some ground. The far right and the far left congressmen and senators skittered away, having been forced to yield to the resounding majority. Each party supplied the necessary votes: In the House, 144 Republicans joined 165 Democrats to pass the bill, officially named the "Fiscal Responsibility Act of 2023." And yet, there were still 70 Republicans who voted no, as did 46 Dems.

In the Senate, Majority Leader Chuck Schumer mustered 46 votes. He was joined by Minority Leader Mitch McConnell, who had 17 Republican votes. Together they forged a filibuster-avoiding majority.

This was an historic achievement, particularly given the vitriolic battles that the extremes of each party have been waging. It seemed to me that when the moment came, the leaders figuratively high-fived, took a breath and moved on. Perhaps they felt that the "clowns on the left" and the "jokers on the right" might cool off and move on rather than wallowing in their despair.

Because a bi-partisan action took place, we didn't have to speculate about how wide and deep such a catastrophic financial occurrence might have been.

Should we feel that optimistic about avoiding a travesty like that one? Should we rejoice because enough good people came together to prevent a calamity? Maybe not. But, it keeps the flames of hope flickering. Hopefully, after the election in 2024 there will be more reasonable, and, dare I say, moderate people elected from both parties, allowing America to fulfill its destiny for all people.

Maybe reasonable leaders from both parties can consider the "nuclear option" of joining together by crossing party lines to nominate moderate candidates. It has been done. I did it and lightning didn't strike. When I was a youngster growing up in Republican East Tennessee, and when the GOP wanted to have a say in *who* was the Volunteer State's governor.... they did what might be unthinkable today: They crossed party lines to vote in the Democratic primary. Maybe fellow Dems will consider finding allies and crossing over to assist moderate candidates in winning elections today? This situation exists and goes both ways in countless states. Don't expend precious energy yearning for a third party; we simply need to work smarter with the two parties we already have.

I may not be around to see it, but it is my hope for my kids, my grandkids, and my great-grandkids...and yours, that they will all experience the kind of freedoms that many Americans have come to take so readily for granted.

X. A RENEWING OF IMPERFECT AMERICA'S VOWS.
A NEW DECLARATION OF INDEPENDENCE

As imperfect citizens we should renew our imperfect vows
Couples quite often use milestone anniversaries to renew their vows, even when the couple and the marriage isn't 100% perfect. And, yet, they continue to celebrate the good while believing that there will be better times ahead.

In less than 1000 days, our nation will arrive at a monumental milestone. On July 4, 2026, we will observe and, hopefully, commemorate America's 250th anniversary. More than two centuries ago, that pesky, almost inconceivable Declaration of Independence set off a chain of unexpected events including: wars with others, wars with ourselves, famines, depressions, threats from others and threats from ourselves, along with waves of hate and prejudice. Amazingly, we not only survived it all, but during the process became the most prosperous, peaceful, powerful country in the world.

I'm proposing that we should set a deadline for our United States to come together as never before: An imperfect people seeking imperfect solutions. The ideal time? Why 07/04/2026, of course.

If we can agree to at least start with one of the most powerful declarations in history, I'm banking on our chances for the future. Here's my suggestion for the updated vow that we should make:

We hold these truths to be self-evident, that all PEOPLE are created equal, that they are endowed by their CREATORS with certain inalienable Rights, that among these are Life, Liberty and the pursuit of Happiness...we mutually pledge to each other our Life, our Fortune, and our sacred Honor.

As I was wrapping these thoughts up, I reflected on the many pleasant, interesting, meandering discussions that Johnny Waters and I had while sitting in our lawn chairs. I smiled because I knew that Johnny and his friend, Senator Howard Baker, would have been completely in favor of my idea. They would have also welcomed all of the clowns and every joker into the fold with open arms.

(A CALL TO ACTION: Join a growing number of Americans— of any age—in renewing our vows! Please become a signatory of the updated Declaration of Independence. I am requesting that as many individuals as possible become a permanent part of this document by July 4, 2026, which is when our nation will

observe and celebrate the 250th Anniversary of this incredible experiment called "Democracy." A complete list of all signees will be permanently maintained. Though there is absolutely no cost or obligation, I am hopeful that everyone signing agrees to honor and celebrate these principals. Participating is simple. Just visit **flamingmoderatebook.com**. *Thank you.)*

ACKNOWLEDGMENTS

It takes a village to produce a book. In my case there are multiple villages to cite in order to credit the many people who directly contributed to the book itself, and to so many others who are, or were, a part of my life and influenced me. This is my attempt to recognize them and say thank you.

THE BOOK VILLAGE

Directly involved thanks goes to my partners, critics, and confidants Andy Roberts, Aldo Amato, and my editor, Leigh Hendry (more about her later); the outstanding help and guidance from wiser-than-his-age Zach Bates, tough critic and friend Ken Renner, and John Butler, for the international historical perspective, and once again, my author mentor Andrew Maraniss. The patient guidance from my author manager at Gatekeeper Press, Trinity Nirenberg. And, in a repeat performance, Cyndy Waters, a gifted photographer, researcher, and beloved friend, and to photographers and friends Jerry Atnip and Jed DeKalb.

Much of this book is made up of op-ed columns first published in the Nashville Tennessean, and I want to thank the exceptional professionals there with whom I worked over the years... I consider them friends: Sandra Roberts, Terry Quillen, John Gibson, Dwight Lewis, and David Plazas. I also want to thank the other publications which helped give life to my columns as well.

THE FAMILY VILLAGE

Special thanks for the love and support from Sam and Tammy Roberts, Andy Roberts, Mark and Mary Roberts, grandchildren Drew, Haley, Haden, Parker, Abbey, Annie Jo, and Cameron, along with their wonderful spouses and significant others, Josh Bilbrey, Bianca Fuchs, Jessica Simpson, Braxton Kinlaw, and Tryston Hayes; my great grandchildren Copeland, Ethan and Jasper, Rayne, and Anderson. Also, my brother Gary and his wife Mary Evelyn, my niece Tracy and her husband, Kevin O'Connor and their children and their families: Keith and Kelly, their children, Kaden and Kayla, and Wesley and Ashley O'Connor.

And, my add-on family, thanks to Leigh, who so enriches our lives: Leslie Holm, Seth and Mary Clare Holm, Turner and Karina Holm, Annie and Brown Dennis, and their children, respectively, Helen, Alice, and Sutherland V, Julia and William, and Townsend (aka "Ella T") and Wylie; Nelson and Evelyn Hendry; Ginna and Jay Tillman and their daughters and spouses, Kaitlin Tillman, Megan and Kaleb Billingsley, and Sarah and Bennett Neece.

All have provided love, laughter and support. (NOTE: Some exceptions to support when it comes to football teams).

THE FRIENDS VILLAGE
Friends were and are vital in providing support and care and understanding, not just in writing books, but for life itself: Jerry Atnip, Jamie and Reen Baskin, Whitney and Zack Bates, Sarah Silva and Rob Beach, Lady and Billy Bird, Amanda Bledsoe, Toni Bryan, Sandy and Rick Catinella, David and Emma Claiborne, Spencer Bowers and Charlie Clark, Carol and Johnny Fred Coleman, Toby Compton, Melanie and Dave Cooley, Darlene Corbitt, Mandy Cordaro, Steve and Angel Cropper, Tonya Cumbee, Alfred and Tiffany Degrafinreid II, Lois Riggins and David Ezzell, Fletcher Foster, David and Elizabeth Fox, Howard Gentry, Eddie and Laurie Gore, Laura Grider, Katherine and Dan Hartle, Aubrey and Carlana Harwell, Christie and Melissa Hauck, Jim and Jeannie Henry, Kem Hinton, Chuck Welch and Gloria Houghland, Jamie and Karen Isabel, Dana Moore and Jack Isenhour, Justyna Kelly, Connie Kennedy, Sameera Lowe, Betty and Raul Malo, Bert and Brooks Mathews, Denis Maupetit, Gay Maxwell, Herb and Wanda Maxwell, Kaye and Steve Maynard, Jesse Goldstein and Adam Maxwell, Joe McCamish, Doug McCarty, Steve Merrill, Stacie Standifer and Tim Nichols, Jenny and Jeff Pennington, Leslie and Rob Perkins, Trudy Peters, David and Emily Preston, Susie Racek, Jamie Ray, Jeri Ray, Ken and Leslie Renner, Kevin and Katy Rucker, Bill Schmidt, Karl and

Elizabeth Sillay, Cheryl and Joe Strichik, Jon Brock and Lofton Stuart, Edwina Temple, Mary Pat Tyree, Niki Tyree, Georgiana Vines, Ann Ellington and Tim Wagner, Harry Weisiger, and Matt and Mia Welsh.

THE POLITICAL/INFLUENCER/FRIENDS VILLAGE

Writing a book including opinions, I obviously have been affected by many other friends as well. Some of those are mentioned above, but in addition, (over the years) many have had an impact and influence on me, including: Jim Henry, Jimmy Naifeh and Bill Purcell, the founders of the "esteemed" organization called "The Has Beens," made up of folks like them and myself who have played a role in government at some level...a place where acquaintances transform into good friends, such as Hal Hardin, Paul Summers, and Gerald McCormick.

Other political influencers and friends include: Jeff Aiken, Lamar Alexander, Burkley Allen, Cecil Alred, Rogers Anderson, Carol Andrews, James Armistead, Mike Arms, Victor Ashe, Kim Atkins, Greg Atkins, Gordon Ball, Don Baltimore, Megan Barry, Margaret Behm, Regina Bell, Jim Benedict, Melissa Blackburn, David Bohan, Spencer Bowers, Randy Boyd, Bill Bradley, Phil Bredesen, Julie Brewer, David Briley, Betty Brown, Joe Bruner, Kyle Buda, Kim Bumpas, Joe Burchfield, Adam Burke, Kim Dettwiller Burton, Heidi Campbell, Mark Cate, Will Cheek, Chandra Cheeseborough, Harry Christenberry, Pete Claussen,

Frank Clement, Bob Clement, Steve Cohen, Chase Cole, Toby Compton, Lew Conner, Dave Cooley, Jim Cooper, Bob Cooper, Bob Corker, Elizabeth Corker, Dan Crockett, Robert Davidson, Ben Davis, Karl Dean, Marilyn Dillihay, Warren Dockter, Vic Donoho, Spruell Driver, Mike DuBose, Jim Duke, Jimmy Duncan, Winfield Dunn, Wayne Edwards, Butch Eley, Daphne Engel, Pete Ezell, Amy Fair, Monica Fawknotson, Tim Fisher, Chip Forrester, Johnny Franks, Jim Free, Bob Freeman, Jim Friedrich, Bill Frist, Brenda Gadd, Matt Gallivan, Tom Garland, Butch Garrett, Paulette Gayden, Kip Gayden, Howard Gentry, Sharon Gentry, Taylor Gentry, Eddie George, Sheila Gibson, Frank Gibson, Brenda Gilmore, Ron Gobbell, Rodrigo Gomez, Bill Goodwin, Bart Gordon, Al Gore, Lovie Grant, Russ Greene, Jay Grider, Caleb Hemmer, Tre Hargett, Paul Harmon, Paul Harrison, Ed Harvey, Beth Harwell, Bill Haslam, Jim Haslam, Jennifer Hatten, Shelly Hay, Gary Heatherly, Sean Henry, Kem Hinton, Bob Hensley, Steve Hewlett, Holli Hines, Caroline Hipps, Doug Hogreph, Doug Horne, Charles Howorth, Susan Huggins, Keel Hunt, Phillip Hutchison, John Ingram, Tom Ingram, Deana Ivey, Jason Ivey, Bill Jenkins, Matt Joki, Lynda Jones, Bobby Joslin, Christine Karbowiak, Beverly Keel, Mike Keith, Mike Kelly, Ron Kirkland, Matt Kisber, Sydney Bever Kiser, Bill Koch, Rae Krenn, Wayne Lambert, Brad Lampley, Stephen Land, Kevin Lavender, Ellen Lehman, Buddy Lewis, Stephen Lindsay, Kevin Liska, Rick Locker, Anne Locke, Hank Adam Locklin, Mack Lynn,

Pam Martin, Doug Mathews, Holly McCall, Alexis MacAllister, Joyce McDaniels, Willie McDonald, Scott McGillberry, Carroll McMahan, Randy McNally, Mark McNeely, Stuart McWhorter, Richard Montgomery, John Morgan, Jason Mumpower, Kathleen Murphy, Dianne Neal, Tom Neff, Rip Noel, Mike Organ, Freddie O'Connell, Curtis Person, Jennifer Pfeiffer, Teresa Phillips, Paige Pitts, David Plazas, Tammy Poole, Kendall Poole, Joe Powell, Amanda Powell, Lisa Quigley, Sandy Quinn, Tara Rader, Mike Ragsdale, Scott Ramsey, Randy Rayburn, Rich Riebeling, Dave Roberts-The Younger, Mary Carolyn Roberts, Rich Roberts, Ronald Roberts, Sylvia Roberts, Worrick Robinson IV, Theotis Robinson, Patricia Ines Robledo, Mark Rogers, Joe Rogers, Bob Rolfe, John Rose, John Rowley, Nancy Russell, Ron Samuels, Brenda Sanderson, Ruble Sanderson, Karl Schledwitz, Andy Sher, Dale Sims, Stephen Smith, Charles Smith, Butch Spyridon, Billy Stair, Kent Starwalt, Jeff Syracuse, Bill Tate, Debi Tate, Bobby Thomas, Cathy Thomas, Scott Thompson, Byron Trauger, Bob Tuke, Niki Tyree, Mary Pat Tyree, Randy Tyree, Claudia Viken, Gary Wade, Dr. Ming Wang, Ray Waters, Pete Weber, Eddie Weeks, Pete Wein, Phil Wenck, Kay West, Courtney Wheeler, Evette White, Ed White, Carey Whitworth, Vivian Wilhoite, Joey Wilson, Justin Wilson, Toby Wilt, Matt Wiltshire, Stacy Winsatt, Kerry Witcher, Laura Womack, Yvonne Wood, Brenda Wynn, Stacy Yarborough, and Jeff Yarbro.

I am sure I missed many, and I didn't use titles because so many have had multiple ....such as State Rep., Speaker of the House, Congressman, and Judge Bill Jenkins.

THE POSTHUMOUS VILLAGE

I have included a few friends who were still with us when I started this column-writing journey. All had an influence on my political views, life, and opinions:

Jerry Adams, Charles Appleton, Clare Armistead, Ben Atchley, Fred Atchley, Howard Baker, Dick Barry, Ray Bell, Ed Boling, Leonard Bradley, Bob Church, Betty Davis, Emmett Edwards, Mason Goodman, Doug Henry, Roy Herron, Tom Jackson, Tom Jensen, Walter Lambert, H.T. Lockhart, Harlan Mathews, Ned McWherter, Clayton McWhorter, Kitty Moon, Jim Neal, Bill Nunnelly, Steve Oglesby, Ben Rechter, Charles Sargent, John Seigenthaler, Bill Snodgrass, Don Sundquist, Fred Thompson, Twyman Towery, Johnny Waters, John Wilder and John Word.

THE HOWARD BAKER VILLAGE

Those close to my "hero" who I had the privilege of knowing through him: Top aide Tommy Griscom and early young staffer Lamar Alexander, and no longer with us: friend and campaign manager Johnny Waters, pilot and philosopher Lonnie Strunk, scribe Lee Smith, solid Bill Hamby, barracuda Ron McMahan, token Democrat law partner and exceptional friend Bob Worthington, steadfast Frank Barnett, partner-in-so-many- ways Lewis Donelson, and fundraiser/mentor par excellence Bill Swaim.

THE LARGEST VILLAGE OF ONE

There's no thanks big enough for my best friend, Leigh, who happens to also be the love of my life and the planet's finest editor. Quite a combo. On behalf of myself and our now departed, yet inspirational, Turner the D.O.G. and Buttah the Rescue Dawg, thanks, Babe.